SALADS, PASTA AND VEGETABLES

◆

D1634470

Reader's Digest Healthy Cooking Library

SALADS, PASTA AND VEGETABLES

Reader's
Digest

Published by The Reader's Digest Association Limited

LONDON ◆ NEW YORK ◆ SYDNEY ◆ CAPE TOWN ◆ MONTREAL

The Reader's Digest Healthy Cooking Library was edited and
designed by The Reader's Digest Association Ltd, London.
These recipes and illustrations have previously appeared in
GREAT RECIPES FOR GOOD HEALTH, published in 1993
by Reader's Digest, UK.

First Edition

Copyright © 1995
The Reader's Digest Association Limited,
Berkeley Square House,
Berkeley Square,
London W1X 6AB.
Copyright © 1995
Reader's Digest Association Far East Limited.
Philippines Copyright © 1995
Reader's Digest Association Far East Limited.

All rights reserved.
No part of this book may be reproduced, stored in a retrieval
system, or transmitted in any form or by any means, electronic,
electrostatic, magnetic tape, mechanical, photocopying,
recording or otherwise, without permission in writing
from the publishers.

® Reader's Digest, The Digest and the Pegasus logo are
registered trademarks of The Reader's Digest Association, Inc,
of Pleasantville, New York, USA.

Printed in Italy

ISBN 0 276 42174 4

Consultant Editor Pat Alburey
Nutritional Consultant Editor Cynthia Robinson, BSc
Nutritional Consultant Moya de Wet, BSc, SRD

Recipes created by Pat Alburey, Valerie Barrett, Jackie Burrow,
Carole Handslip, Petra Jackson, Meg Jansz, Angela Kingsbury,
Danielle Nay, Louise Pickford, Jane Suthering, Judith Taylor,
Hilaire Walden

CONTENTS

SALADS

Salad days can fall on any day of the year now that most fresh vegetables are in the shops all the year round. Forget about limp lettuce and insipid tomatoes; salads can be much more interesting. Light and crunchy green salads, crisped in the refrigerator and tossed in a little low-fat dressing make the perfect accompaniment to main dishes, while a variety of raw and cooked vegetables can become almost an appetising meal on their own, especially when they include some meat, fish, pasta or cheese.

Artichoke, broccoli and cheese salad

ONE SERVING	
CALORIES	95
TOTAL FAT	6g
SATURATED FAT	2g
CARBOHYDRATES	6g
ADDED SUGAR	0
FIBRE	3g
SODIUM	55mg

SERVES 4
PREPARATION TIME: 20 minutes
COOKING TIME: 5 minutes

4oz (115g) Jerusalem artichokes, peeled and
thinly sliced
1 teaspoon lemon juice
8oz (225g) broccoli, trimmed and divided
into florets

1 tablespoon virgin olive oil
1½ teaspoons balsamic vinegar or red wine vinegar
1 level tablespoon fresh tarragon leaves,
or 1 level teaspoon dried tarragon
Freshly ground black pepper
6 cherry tomatoes, cut in half
6oz (175g) tinned artichoke hearts, well rinsed,
drained and cut in half
1oz (30g) mozzarella cheese, cut into small cubes

Jerusalem and globe artichokes, different in texture but similar in taste, blend with sweet tomatoes and gentle mozzarella to mellow the broccoli.

1 Cook the Jerusalem artichoke slices in
unsalted boiling water, with the lemon juice
added, for 2-3 minutes, until just becoming
tender. Rinse in a colander under cold water
and drain well.

2 Meanwhile, steam the broccoli for about
4 minutes, until slightly softened but still crisp.
Rinse in a colander under cold running water
and drain well.

3 Combine the oil with the vinegar and
tarragon, and season with pepper. Gently stir
in the broccoli, tomatoes, artichoke hearts,
Jerusalem artichokes and mozzarella, taking
care not to break the broccoli florets.

Serve the salad at once, or cover it and
refrigerate for up to 1 hour if more convenient;
turn the salad again just before serving. It
goes particularly well with grilled fish.

Aubergine salad

SERVES 4
PREPARATION TIME: 15 minutes, plus 1 hour to stand and 5 hours to cool and refrigerate
COOKING TIME: 30 minutes
OVEN: Preheat to 200°C (400°F, gas mark 6)

ONE SERVING	
CALORIES	100
TOTAL FAT	8g
SATURATED FAT	1g
CARBOHYDRATES	5g
ADDED SUGAR	0
FIBRE	3g
SODIUM	250mg

Baking gives aubergines a melting texture and full, nutty flavour. This is enhanced by the oil and herb dressing which penetrates the aubergine fans.

8 small aubergines, about 1¼ lb (550g) together
½ level teaspoon salt
8oz (225g) ripe tomatoes, skinned, de-seeded and diced
3 cloves garlic, peeled and crushed
1 level tablespoon chopped fresh parsley
1 level tablespoon chopped fresh coriander
6 tablespoons water
Freshly ground black pepper
2 tablespoons virgin olive oil
Sprigs of fresh coriander to garnish

1 Slice the aubergines thinly from the tip towards the stalk, leaving the slices joined at the stalk end. Leave the stalk in place but trim it of any prickly bristles.

2 Put the aubergines in a wide dish, sprinkle with the salt and leave for 1 hour for the bitter juices to be drawn out. Meanwhile, mix the tomatoes with the garlic, parsley and coriander.

3 Rinse the aubergines well with cold water and pat dry with kitchen paper. Arrange them close together in an ovenproof dish and spread a little of the tomato mixture between the slices. Pour in the water and season with pepper. Trickle the oil over the aubergines. Cover and cook in the heated oven for 30 minutes or until soft, basting occasionally.

4 Remove from the oven, leave to cool, then refrigerate for 4 hours while the flavour develops. Serve garnished with the coriander.

When small aubergines are unavailable, use four medium ones. Halve them lengthways, then place cut side down and slice thinly as for small aubergines.

Avocado, bean and cucumber salad

ONE SERVING

CALORIES 155

TOTAL FAT 13g

SATURATED FAT 2g

CARBOHYDRATES 6g

ADDED SUGAR 0

FIBRE 5g

SODIUM 65mg

The creamy texture and subtle taste of avocado contrast with crisp cucumber and beans in a salad that is an ideal partner for prawns.

SERVES 4
PREPARATION TIME: 20 minutes
COOKING TIME: 5 minutes

6oz (175g) shelled or frozen broad beans
6oz (175g) bobby or pencil beans, trimmed and cut into short lengths
¼ cucumber, peeled, halved lengthways and sliced
1 tablespoon lemon juice
1 level teaspoon Dijon mustard
1 tablespoon virgin olive oil
1 level tablespoon chopped fresh parsley
1 level tablespoon chopped fresh chervil
Freshly ground black pepper
1 ripe avocado halved, stoned, peeled and quartered
Parsley sprigs to garnish

1 Cook the broad beans and bobby or pencil beans in unsalted boiling water for 4 minutes, until just tender. Rinse, drain and cool slightly.

2 Pop the inner part of the broad beans from the outer skins by gently squeezing each bean between a thumb and forefinger. Put all the beans into a bowl with the cucumber.

3 Whisk the lemon juice, mustard, oil and herbs together, and season with pepper. Pour over the vegetables and toss well.

4 Cut the avocado quarters across into slices and stir into the salad. Garnish with parsley sprigs and serve at once.

> **TIP**
> *Prepare the avocado and mix it into the salad just before serving. If it is prepared too soon, it will discolour.*

Green bean and courgette salad

ONE SERVING

CALORIES 55

TOTAL FAT 4g

SATURATED FAT 1g

CARBOHYDRATES 3g

ADDED SUGAR 0

FIBRE 2g

SODIUM 5mg

SERVES 4
PREPARATION TIME: 25 minutes
COOKING TIME: 2 minutes

8oz (225g) fine green beans, trimmed and halved
1 tablespoon virgin olive oil
1 clove garlic, peeled and crushed
½ level teaspoon dried tarragon
Freshly ground black pepper
1 medium courgette, cut into matchstick strips
1 small red onion, peeled and chopped
1½ teaspoons tarragon-flavoured vinegar

1 Cook the beans, in just enough unsalted boiling water to cover, for 2-3 minutes, until slightly softened but still crisp. Pour into a colander, rinse with cold water, then drain.

2 Mix the oil, garlic and tarragon, and season with pepper. Stir in the beans, courgette and onion, and turn until coated. Serve at once sprinkled with the vinegar or, if you prefer, cover and chill in the refrigerator for 1 hour; toss the salad and sprinkle with the vinegar just before serving.

Mixed bean salad

ONE SERVING

CALORIES 125

TOTAL FAT 5g

SATURATED FAT 1g

CARBOHYDRATES 15g

ADDED SUGAR 0

FIBRE 5g

SODIUM 20mg

*Beans are versatile
ingredients for salads.
Fresh green beans are
tossed with courgettes in
tarragon dressing (left),
while dried beans make
a colourful mix with
celery, red pepper and
firm button mushrooms.*

SERVES 4
PREPARATION TIME: 10 minutes
COOKING TIME: 5-8 minutes

1 large red pepper
2oz (60g) fine green beans, trimmed and halved
*1 small red onion, peeled and thinly sliced,
or 2 spring onions, trimmed and thinly sliced*
*3oz (85g) cooked cannellini beans or black-eyed
beans (see p.17)*
3oz (85g) cooked flageolet beans
3oz (85g) cooked red kidney beans
2 sticks celery, trimmed and thinly sliced
2oz (60g) button mushrooms, wiped and sliced
1 tablespoon virgin olive oil
1 tablespoon lemon juice
1 level tablespoon chopped fresh parsley
Freshly ground black pepper

1 Grill the red pepper under a moderate heat,
turning often, for 5-8 minutes, until the skin
blisters. Put the pepper in a bowl, cover with a
damp cloth and leave for about 5 minutes.

2 Meanwhile, cook the green beans, in just
enough unsalted boiling water to cover, for
2-3 minutes, or until slightly softened but still
crisp. Rinse with cold water and drain.

3 Peel and de-seed the pepper, working
over a bowl to catch any juices. Slice the pepper
lengthways into strips.

4 Mix all the ingredients, including the pepper
juice, and season with black pepper. Serve at
once, or cover and chill in the refrigerator for
2 hours if preferred; mix again before serving.

Bean sprout salad

SERVES 4
PREPARATION TIME: 10 minutes, plus 1 hour
to refrigerate

ONE SERVING	
CALORIES 60	
TOTAL FAT 4g	
SATURATED FAT 0	
CARBOHYDRATES 4g	
ADDED SUGAR 0	
FIBRE 1g	
SODIUM 10mg	

1 tablespoon sesame or peanut oil
2 spring onions, trimmed and chopped
1 level teaspoon tomato purée
1 clove garlic, peeled and crushed
2 level teaspoons peeled and grated root ginger
8oz (225g) bean sprouts, rinsed and drained
1 small red pepper, de-seeded and thinly sliced
1½ teaspoons lemon juice
1½ teaspoons rice vinegar or white wine vinegar

1 Combine the oil, onions, tomato purée, garlic and ginger in a small saucepan, and stir over a low heat for about 1 minute, or until the mixture starts to bubble. Remove from the heat and leave the dressing until cold.

2 Mix the bean sprouts and red pepper, stir in the dressing and toss well. Cover and chill in the refrigerator for 1 hour, tossing occasionally.

3 Just before serving, stir in the lemon juice and vinegar, toss again and spoon the salad into a serving bowl.

Pickled beetroot salad

ONE SERVING	
CALORIES 70	
TOTAL FAT 0	
SATURATED FAT 0	
CARBOHYDRATES 14g	
ADDED SUGAR 0	
FIBRE 4g	
SODIUM 160mg	

SERVES 4
PREPARATION TIME: 20 minutes, plus 2 hours
to refrigerate
COOKING TIME: 1 hour 30 minutes

6 medium beetroots, about 1½ lb (680g) together, washed and with tops trimmed to 1in (25mm)
4fl oz (115ml) water
4fl oz (115ml) cider vinegar
2 level teaspoons freshly grated horseradish
1 level teaspoon Dijon mustard
6 black peppercorns
4 cloves
1 bay leaf
2 spring onions, trimmed and chopped
1 level tablespoon chopped fresh dill or fennel fronds

1 Put the beetroots in a large, uncovered saucepan of unsalted boiling water and simmer them for 1 hour 30 minutes, or until tender. Drain and leave to cool. Top and tail and peel the beetroots. Cut them into slices and arrange the slices in a heatproof dish.

2 Bring the water, vinegar, horseradish, mustard, peppercorns, cloves and bay leaf to the boil. Pour the mixture over the beetroot slices and leave to cool. Cover and chill in the refrigerator for 2 hours.

3 Just before serving, remove the bay leaf and cloves, and sprinkle the salad with the spring onions and dill or fennel.

TIP
Pick beetroots with undamaged skin and avoid damage while washing and trimming, or colour will bleed out.

Italian-style bread and tomato salad

ONE SERVING	
CALORIES 260	
TOTAL FAT 13g	
SATURATED FAT 2g	
CARBOHYDRATES 30g	
ADDED SUGAR 0	
FIBRE 5g	
SODIUM 340mg	

SERVES 4
PREPARATION TIME: 20 minutes, plus 2-3 hours
to refrigerate

8oz (225g) stale wholemeal or white bread, with crusts cut off
4 tablespoons water
4 large ripe tomatoes, skinned, de-seeded and diced
1 small cucumber, peeled and sliced
1 stick celery, trimmed and chopped
1 small onion, peeled and finely chopped
1 level teaspoon capers, rinsed and drained

1 large sprig fresh basil leaves, finely shredded
Freshly ground black pepper
3 tablespoons virgin olive oil
1 tablespoon lemon juice or wine vinegar
1 level tablespoon chopped celery leaves

1 Cut the bread into thick slices and spread them in a wide dish. Sprinkle with the water and leave to stand for 5-10 minutes.

2 Tear the bread into small pieces. Mix in the tomatoes, cucumber, celery, onion, capers and

Beetroot slices in a pungent mustard and horseradish marinade create a sweet and sour salad of vibrant colour. An Italian salad of bread and tomatoes (top), sharpened with capers and basil, makes unusual and delicious use of stale bread. Bean sprouts match the sweetness of red pepper in a low-calorie salad dressed in an Oriental style.

TIP
After tearing up the moist bread, toss it with a fork to increase the volume as much as possible.

basil. Season with pepper and pour on the oil. Cover and put in the refrigerator for 2-3 hours for the bread to absorb the dressing.

3 Sprinkle the lemon juice or vinegar over the salad and spoon into a serving dish. Stir in the celery leaves just before serving.

Broccoli and sesame salad

ONE SERVING

CALORIES 105

TOTAL FAT 6g

SATURATED FAT 1g

CARBOHYDRATES 4g

ADDED SUGAR 1g

FIBRE 5g

SODIUM 200mg

SERVES 4
PREPARATION TIME: 15 minutes
COOKING TIME: 5 minutes

1½ lb (680g) broccoli, cut into small florets and
thick stems cut off, peeled and coarsely chopped
2 teaspoons soy sauce
2 tablespoons white wine vinegar
2 teaspoons sesame oil or peanut oil
½ teaspoon clear honey
1 level tablespoon sesame seeds, lightly toasted

1 Steam the broccoli for 5 minutes, or until cooked through but still firm. Turn it into a serving dish.

2 Mix the soy sauce, vinegar, oil and honey, pour the mixture over the broccoli and toss well. Sprinkle the sesame seeds over the broccoli and serve.

Marinated carrots

ONE SERVING

CALORIES 70

TOTAL FAT 4g

SATURATED FAT 1g

CARBOHYDRATES 8g

ADDED SUGAR 0

FIBRE 2g

SODIUM 30mg

SERVES 4
PREPARATION TIME: 10 minutes, plus 24 hours
to marinate
COOKING TIME: 10 minutes

12oz (340g) young carrots, peeled and cut
into quarters lengthways
7fl oz (200ml) white wine vinegar
4fl oz (115ml) water
1 tablespoon virgin olive oil
2 garlic cloves, peeled and finely chopped
2 level tablespoons chopped fresh oregano,
or 1 level teaspoon dried oregano
Finely chopped carrot leaves or parsley to garnish

1 Cook the carrots in enough unsalted boiling water to cover them, for about 8 minutes or until cooked through but still firm. Drain, turn into a heatproof bowl and set aside.

2 Meanwhile, pour the vinegar and water into a small stainless steel or enamel saucepan and bring to the boil. Boil rapidly, uncovered, until the mixture is reduced by about a half.

3 Mix the oil, garlic and oregano into the carrots, then stir in the vinegar. Leave until cool, then cover and put in the refrigerator for 24 hours.

4 Spoon the carrots into a serving dish and scatter on the carrot leaves or parsley before serving.

This sweet and sour dish is a good partner for cold roast beef or pork.

> **TIP**
> *To give the marinade the best flavour, be sure to boil the vinegar. This gives it a much mellower taste.*

Cauliflower and mushroom salad

ONE SERVING

CALORIES 150

TOTAL FAT 13g

SATURATED FAT 2g

CARBOHYDRATES 4g

ADDED SUGAR 0

FIBRE 3g

SODIUM 20mg

SERVES 4
PREPARATION TIME: 25 minutes

8oz (225g) firm white cauliflower, divided
into florets
Chinese cabbage heart, washed, dried and
finely sliced
8 button mushrooms, wiped and thinly sliced
6 walnut halves, roughly chopped

3 level tablespoons low-fat natural yoghurt
1 teaspoon lemon juice
1½ level tablespoons chopped fresh chervil
or parsley
1 level teaspoon mustard seeds, crushed
1 tablespoon virgin olive oil
2 tablespoons water
Freshly ground black pepper

1 Wash the cauliflower and dry it thoroughly with kitchen paper. Cut the florets lengthways into thin slices.

2 Put the cauliflower, cabbage, mushrooms and walnuts in a salad bowl.

3 Whisk together the yoghurt, lemon juice, chervil or parsley, mustard seeds, oil and water, and season with pepper.

4 Pour the dressing over the salad, mix gently to coat everything lightly, and serve.

Long marination allows tender carrots to absorb the tangy oregano and vinegar dressing. Tart mustard yoghurt gives a light coating to firm cauliflower and mushroom slices topped with walnuts (top). Broccoli is tossed in honeyed soy sauce and scattered with sesame seeds.

Celeriac salad

ONE SERVING

CALORIES 40

TOTAL FAT 2g

SATURATED FAT 1g

CARBOHYDRATES 4g

ADDED SUGAR 0

FIBRE 4g

SODIUM 90mg

SERVES 4
PREPARATION TIME: 15 minutes

Juice of ½ lemon
4 level tablespoons Greek yoghurt
½ level teaspoon mustard powder
¼ level teaspoon caster sugar
12oz (340g) celeriac, peeled and shredded
or coarsely grated
1 small lettuce, washed, drained and chilled

1 Put the lemon juice, yoghurt, mustard and sugar into a large bowl and whisk to combine into a smooth dressing.

2 Mix the celeriac into the dressing, stirring well to coat it.

3 Line four individual salad bowls with lettuce leaves. Spoon the celeriac into the centre and serve at once.

> **TIP**
> *Do not peel and shred the celeriac until the dressing is ready. Add it immediately to the dressing and stir frequently to avoid discoloration.*

A creamy-textured mustard dressing makes a fiery companion for mildly peppery celeriac in a refreshing salad that is easy to prepare.

Citrus fruit and watercress salad

ONE SERVING

CALORIES 170

TOTAL FAT 11g

SATURATED FAT 1g

CARBOHYDRATES 12g

ADDED SUGAR 0

FIBRE 5g

SODIUM 30mg

SERVES 4
PREPARATION TIME: 30 minutes

2 pink grapefruits
2 oranges
1 small cos or iceberg lettuce, trimmed and washed
8oz (225g) watercress, washed and thick
stems removed
1 tablespoon red wine vinegar
2 teaspoons virgin olive oil
6 walnut halves, lightly toasted and
coarsely chopped

1 Using a small sharp knife, remove the peel and all the white pith from the grapefruits and oranges. Hold the fruit over a bowl to catch the juice while you slice between the membrane and the flesh at each side of every segment to cut it free.

2 Put the lettuce leaves into a salad bowl with the watercress. Drain the juice from the grapefruit and orange segments and set it aside. Add the segments to the lettuce and watercress and mix gently.

3 Mix the vinegar and oil with 2 tablespoons of the grapefruit and orange juice. Pour it over the lettuce and watercress, and toss well. Sprinkle on the walnuts and serve at once.

Coleslaw

ONE SERVING

CALORIES 40

TOTAL FAT 1g

SATURATED FAT 0

CARBOHYDRATES 7g

ADDED SUGAR 0

FIBRE 2g

SODIUM 25mg

TIP

Give the coleslaw 2-3 hours to develop and mingle the flavours but do not leave it longer. The cabbages lose their crispness and release a rather bitter juice into the dressing.

SERVES 4
PREPARATION TIME: 15 minutes,
plus 2-3 hours to refrigerate

6 level tablespoons low-fat natural yoghurt
½ small onion, peeled and grated
2 level teaspoons mustard powder mixed with water
¼ level teaspoon caraway seeds
⅛ level teaspoon dried dill weed
Freshly ground black pepper
4oz (115g) white cabbage, finely shredded
4oz (115g) red cabbage, finely shredded
1 small carrot, peeled and coarsely grated

¼ small green pepper, de-seeded and sliced lengthways into thin strips
¼ small red pepper, de-seeded, and sliced lengthways into thin strips

1　Combine the yoghurt, onion, mustard, caraway and dill in a large dish, and season with pepper. Mix in the white and red cabbage, the carrot and the peppers, stirring thoroughly to coat everything with the dressing.

2　Cover the dish and chill in the refrigerator for 2-3 hours, stirring occasionally.

Sweet oranges and sharper grapefruits refresh a green salad and add to the zesty dressing, while mustard and caraway flavour a coleslaw.

Cottage cheese and fruit salad

SERVES 4
PREPARATION TIME: 30 minutes, plus 1 hour
to refrigerate

2 level teaspoons cornflour
2 level teaspoons paprika
1 tablespoon lemon juice
Juice of 3 large oranges
1lb (450g) fresh pineapple, skin, core and
woody eyes removed, flesh cut into cubes
2 oranges, peeled, pith removed, cut into chunks
2 kiwi fruits, peeled and thinly sliced
8oz (225g) fresh strawberries, hulled and sliced
12 small cos lettuce leaves, washed and chilled
10oz (275g) cottage cheese

1 In a stainless steel or enamel saucepan, blend the cornflour and paprika to a smooth cream with the lemon juice, then stir in the orange juice. Stir the mixture as you bring it to the boil over a moderate heat. Simmer the sauce for 2-3 minutes, still continuing to stir, until it has thickened slightly.

2 Pour the sauce into a bowl, leave it to cool, then cover and refrigerate for about 1 hour.

3 Meanwhile, put the pineapple, oranges, kiwi fruits and strawberries into a large bowl, cover and refrigerate.

4 Pour the cold orange sauce over the chilled fruit and mix gently. Line individual salad bowls with the lettuce leaves, spoon cottage cheese into the middle of each bowl and encircle it with fruit and sauce.

ONE SERVING	
CALORIES	215
TOTAL FAT	3g
SATURATED FAT	2g
CARBOHYDRATES	35g
ADDED SUGAR	0
FIBRE	3g
SODIUM	280mg

The sweetness and fragrance of fresh fruit is balanced by the slight acidity of cottage cheese to make a light and colourful summer salad.

Crisp, cool cucumber, juicy melon and fragrant strawberries glisten in a lemon dressing, perfumed with the mild citrus scent of coriander.

Cucumber and fruit salad

ONE SERVING	
CALORIES	80
TOTAL FAT	4g
SATURATED FAT	1g
CARBOHYDRATES	9g
ADDED SUGAR	0
FIBRE	1g
SODIUM	20mg

SERVES 4
PREPARATION TIME: 15 minutes

1 small honeydew melon, halved and de-seeded
1 medium cucumber, scored lengthways with a fork and thinly sliced
5oz (150g) strawberries, hulled and quartered
2 tablespoons lemon juice
1 tablespoon virgin olive oil
⅛ level teaspoon cayenne pepper
2 level tablespoons chopped fresh coriander, or ½ level teaspoon ground coriander
Sprigs of fresh mint or coriander to garnish

1 Slice the melon into wedges and cut the flesh away from the skin. Cut the flesh into cubes and mix it with the cucumber and strawberries in a salad bowl.

2 Combine the lemon juice and oil with the cayenne pepper and chopped or ground coriander. Pour the dressing over the fruits and turn to coat everything. Garnish with the mint or coriander sprigs.

You can use any other small ripe melon to make this refreshing dish.

Spicy cucumber and red pepper salad

ONE SERVING

CALORIES 45

TOTAL FAT 3g

SATURATED FAT 0

CARBOHYDRATES 3g

ADDED SUGAR 0

FIBRE 1g

SODIUM 20mg

SERVES 4
PREPARATION TIME: 10 minutes

4 level tablespoons low-fat natural or Greek yoghurt
2 teaspoons sesame or peanut oil
1 tablespoon cider vinegar
½ level teaspoon peeled and grated root ginger,
or ¼ level teaspoon ground ginger
¼ level teaspoon ground coriander
1 large cucumber, halved, quartered lengthways,
de-seeded and cut into thin strips
1 small red pepper, de-seeded and cut into strips
¼ level teaspoon cumin seeds

1 Blend the yoghurt, oil, vinegar, ginger and coriander to make the dressing.

2 Mix the cucumber with the pepper in a salad bowl, spoon on the dressing, sprinkle with the cumin seeds and serve at once. If you prefer, mix the salad thoroughly and chill for 1-2 hours in the refrigerator before serving.

Fennel and cabbage salad

ONE SERVING

CALORIES 65

TOTAL FAT 5g

SATURATED FAT 1g

CARBOHYDRATES 5g

ADDED SUGAR 0

FIBRE 4g

SODIUM 15mg

SERVES 4
PREPARATION TIME: 20 minutes,
plus 15 minutes to stand

2 tablespoons cider vinegar
1 tablespoon virgin olive oil
1 tablespoon white wine
1 level tablespoon cumin seeds, crushed
2 level tablespoons chopped fresh parsley
Freshly ground black pepper
1 medium bulb fennel
12oz (340g) white cabbage, trimmed and
finely shredded
Fennel or dill fronds to garnish

1 Whisk the vinegar, oil and white wine with the cumin seeds and parsley in a salad bowl.

2 Trim off the top and root from the fennel bulb. Discard the outer fennel leaves and cut the bulb in half lengthways. Cut across the halves to give fine slices and put the slices into the dressing.

3 Add the cabbage to the salad, season with pepper and toss the salad thoroughly to combine everything.

4 Cover the salad and leave it to stand for 15 minutes. Garnish it with the fennel or dill fronds just before serving.

This crunchy salad with its slight flavour of aniseed goes particularly well with fish and pasta dishes.

> **TIP**
> **Put the fennel slices into the dressing as you cut them so they do not discolour.**

Fusilli salad with peppers and basil

ONE SERVING

CALORIES 225

TOTAL FAT 4g

SATURATED FAT 2g

CARBOHYDRATES 40g

ADDED SUGAR 0

FIBRE 3g

SODIUM 210mg

SERVES 4
PREPARATION TIME: 15 minutes,
plus 30 minutes to stand
COOKING TIME: 10 minutes

6oz (175g) fusilli
1 large red pepper
1 large yellow pepper
1 clove garlic, peeled and finely chopped
10 basil leaves, finely shredded
½ level teaspoon finely chopped fresh thyme
2 level teaspoons capers, rinsed and drained
1oz (30g) Parmesan cheese, finely chopped
or grated
2 level tablespoons Greek yoghurt
1 level tablespoon seedless raisins
½ level teaspoon paprika
1 level tablespoon snipped chives
Basil sprigs and whole chive stems to garnish

1 Cook the fusilli , and rinse with cold water. Drain thoroughly and set aside.

TIP
If you have time, soak the raisins in 2 tablespoons of cold water for 1 hour before adding them to the salad. Soaking makes them plump and juicy.

2 Grill the peppers under a moderate heat for 10 minutes, turning them frequently until all sides are blistered. Put the peppers in a small bowl, cover with a clean damp cloth and leave for 5 minutes.

3 Peel and de-seed the peppers, working over a bowl to catch the juices. Blend the peppers and their juices into a purée, using a food processor or food mill.

4 Mix the garlic, shredded basil, thyme, capers and Parmesan into the purée, then stir in the yoghurt and raisins.

5 Put the fusilli into a serving bowl, pour on the dressing and mix well until all the spirals are coated with dressing. Sprinkle with the paprika and chives, and garnish with the basil sprigs and chive stems. Cover and leave to stand for 30 minutes before serving.

Aniseed-scented fennel offers a contrasting flavour to the cabbage but matches its texture in a crisp salad (below left). Fusilli – spirals of pasta – add body and raisins sweeten a well-seasoned red pepper purée. Spiced yoghurt with high notes of ginger, coriander and cumin tops colourful strips of cucumber and red pepper.

Greek salad

ONE SERVING
....
CALORIES 120
....
TOTAL FAT 8g
....
   SATURATED FAT 3g
....
CARBOHYDRATES 4g
....
   ADDED SUGAR 0
....
FIBRE 2g
....
SODIUM 400mg
....

SERVES 4
PREPARATION TIME: 20 minutes

½ cos lettuce, trimmed and washed
8oz (225g) young spinach leaves, trimmed
and washed
½ small cucumber, diced
2oz (60g) cottage cheese
2oz (60g) fetta cheese, rinsed with cold water
and cut into small pieces
2 level tablespoons chopped fresh mint,
or 1½ level teaspoons dried mint
1 teaspoon virgin olive oil
1 teaspoon lemon juice
1 clove garlic, peeled and crushed
2 medium black olives, stoned and sliced
Freshly ground black pepper

1 Dry the lettuce and spinach leaves gently
with kitchen paper and tear them into small
pieces. Mix with the cucumber, cottage cheese,
fetta and mint in a salad bowl.

2 Blend the oil with the lemon juice and
garlic, mix in the olives and season with pepper.
Pour the dressing over the salad, toss and serve.

Lamb's lettuce and beetroot salad

ONE SERVING
....
CALORIES 65
....
TOTAL FAT 4g
....
   SATURATED FAT 1g
....
CARBOHYDRATES 5g
....
   ADDED SUGAR 0
....
FIBRE 2g
....
SODIUM 40mg
....

SERVES 4
PREPARATION TIME: 15 minutes

8oz (225g) cooked beetroots, peeled and sliced
3 tablespoons red wine vinegar
1 tablespoon virgin olive oil
1 clove garlic, peeled and finely chopped
Freshly ground black pepper
8oz (225g) lamb's lettuce, trimmed and washed

1 Put the beetroot in a glass bowl, sprinkle
the vinegar on it, cover and leave to stand for
10 minutes. Drain off and discard the vinegar.

2 Combine the oil and garlic in a salad bowl
and season with pepper. Mix in the lamb's
lettuce and beetroot, and serve immediately.

Serve with striped Italian bread for colour.

Oriental mushroom salad

ONE SERVING
....
CALORIES 50
....
TOTAL FAT 4g
....
   SATURATED FAT 0
....
CARBOHYDRATES 3g
....
   ADDED SUGAR 2g
....
FIBRE 1g
....
SODIUM 190mg
....

SERVES 4
PREPARATION TIME: 10 minutes,
plus 20 minutes to refrigerate

1 clove garlic, cut in half
1 teaspoon clear honey
2 teaspoons soy sauce
¼ level teaspoon ground ginger
2 teaspoons red wine vinegar
2 teaspoons sesame or peanut oil
8oz (225g) button mushrooms, wiped and trimmed
1 small yellow pepper, de-seeded and diced
8 radishes, trimmed, washed and sliced
2 level teaspoons chopped fresh coriander or parsley
1 level teaspoon sesame seeds

1 Rub the inside of a large bowl with the
half-cloves of garlic. Whisk the honey, soy
sauce, ginger, vinegar and oil in the bowl.

2 Slice the mushrooms very thinly and add to
the dressing with the pepper and radishes. Toss
well, cover and refrigerate for 20 minutes.

3 Spoon the salad onto a serving plate,
sprinkle with the coriander or parsley and the
sesame seeds, and serve at once.

*The slight bitterness of lamb's lettuce makes it a
perfect foil for crimson slices of sweet beetroot.
Spinach and lettuce form a leafy base for mild
cheeses mixed with salty olives (far right). Honey,
ginger and soy sauce give a taste of the East to
crisp sliced and diced vegetables.*

Pineapple salad

SERVES 4
PREPARATION TIME: 25 minutes

ONE SERVING	
CALORIES	85
TOTAL FAT	4g
SATURATED FAT	1g
CARBOHYDRATES	11g
ADDED SUGAR	0
FIBRE	2g
SODIUM	10mg

Mouthwatering chunks of pineapple add their unique sweet but tangy juiciness to a tomato and green pepper salad and create a refreshing, vividly coloured medley.

*1 clove garlic, peeled and crushed
1 level teaspoon English mustard powder
1 tablespoon lemon juice
Freshly ground black pepper
1 tablespoon virgin olive oil
4 medium tomatoes
1 medium green pepper, quartered and de-seeded
½ medium pineapple
4 small sprigs mint or watercress to garnish*

1 Blend the garlic and mustard, stir in the lemon juice and season with black pepper. Whisk in the oil vigorously until the dressing thickens slightly.

2 Drop the tomatoes and green pepper into boiling water for 1 minute, then rinse with cold water and drain.

3 Skin the tomatoes and cut them into thin wedges. Slice the pepper thinly. Turn the tomatoes and pepper gently in the dressing until coated.

4 Slice the pineapple into thick rings, cut off all the hard skin and prise out the woody 'eyes' with the tip of a knife. Cut the rings in half, trim out the hard centre and slice the flesh into chunks.

5 Mix the pineapple in with the tomatoes and pepper and garnish the dish with the sprigs of mint or watercress. Serve at once.

This sweet but sharp salad goes particularly well with ham and cold pork. You can use unsweetened tinned pineapple chunks instead of fresh pineapple, but the chunks need to be drained well on kitchen paper before being added to the salad.

TIP
Cut the pineapple and mix it into the salad just before serving. If added earlier, it releases too much juice and dilutes the dressing.

Potato, artichoke and red pepper salad

SERVES 4
PREPARATION TIME: 30 minutes,
plus 30 minutes to stand
COOKING TIME: 20 minutes

2 large globe artichokes
4 tablespoons fresh lemon juice
12oz (340g) new potatoes, scrubbed and
thickly sliced
1 large red pepper, halved and de-seeded
3½ oz (100g) set low-fat natural yoghurt
1 level teaspoon Dijon mustard
2 level tablespoons chopped fresh coriander
2 level teaspoons poppy seeds
Freshly ground black pepper
Coriander leaves to garnish

1 Break off the stalk from each artichoke, flush with the base. Pull off the outer layers of leaves, starting from the bottom, until you reach the pale inner leaves, pulling each leaf outwards and downwards until it snaps off.

2 Cut off the pointed top of each artichoke about 1½ in (40mm) above the base, then trim off the dark part from each artichoke base and brush the bases with lemon juice.

3 Using a teaspoon or grapefruit knife, scrape out and discard the hairy choke from the centre of each artichoke. Trim off any remaining dark green parts from the tops and brush the tops with lemon juice.

4 Set aside two teaspoons of the lemon juice and add the remainder to a saucepan of unsalted boiling water. Cook the artichoke hearts in it for about 15 minutes, or until tender, then drain.

5 Meanwhile, steam the potato slices for about 10 minutes, until tender, then cool.

6 While the potatoes cook, grill the pepper halves, skin side up, under a moderate heat for 5-6 minutes, until they blister. Put them in a bowl and cover with a clean damp cloth.

7 Combine the yoghurt, mustard, chopped coriander, poppy seeds and reserved lemon juice, and season with pepper. Slice the artichoke hearts, mix with the potato slices and pour the dressing over them.

8 Peel the skin off the pepper, slice the flesh into strips and scatter on top of the salad. Cover and stand in a cool place for 30 minutes. Garnish with the coriander leaves to serve.

ONE SERVING	
CALORIES	95
TOTAL FAT	2g
SATURATED FAT	1g
CARBOHYDRATES	20g
ADDED SUGAR	0
FIBRE	2g
SODIUM	90mg

Tender slices of artichoke and potato served with an aromatic mustard and coriander dressing are topped with brilliant strips of smoky grilled pepper.

Prawn and fetta salad

SERVES 4
PREPARATION TIME: 20 minutes
COOKING TIME: 5 minutes

ONE SERVING	
CALORIES	165
TOTAL FAT	7g
SATURATED FAT	2g
CARBOHYDRATES	7g
ADDED SUGAR	0
FIBRE	2g
SODIUM	235mg

> **TIP**
> *Always rinse fetta cheese well under cold running water before using it. This mild sheep's-milk cheese is preserved in brine – which greatly increases its salt content if not rinsed off.*

1 large red pepper, halved and de-seeded
1lb (450g) frozen uncooked freshwater prawns, thawed, shelled and de-veined
3 spring onions, trimmed and thinly sliced
½ medium cucumber, peeled and chopped
2 level tablespoons chopped fresh dill or parsley
1oz (30g) fetta cheese, rinsed and crumbled
2 tablespoons lemon juice
1 tablespoon virgin olive oil
1 tablespoon white wine vinegar
1 level teaspoon Dijon mustard
1 clove garlic, peeled and crushed
Freshly ground black pepper
8oz (225g) frisée lettuce, washed and dried
Lemon wedges to garnish

1 Grill the pepper halves, skin side up, under a moderate heat for 5-6 minutes until blistered all over. Put the halves in a small bowl and cover with a clean damp cloth.

2 Bring 2 pints (1.15 litres) of unsalted water to the boil in a large saucepan and cook the prawns in it over a moderate heat, stirring continuously, for about 2 minutes, until they are just firm. Rinse the prawns in a colander under cold running water, drain them and pat dry with kitchen paper.

3 Mix the prawns with the onions, cucumber, dill or parsley and fetta.

4 Pull the skin off the pepper, working over a bowl to catch any juices. Slice the pepper flesh thinly and add it to the prawn mixture.

5 Whisk together the lemon juice, oil, vinegar, juice from the pepper, mustard and garlic until the mixture thickens slightly, then season with

black pepper. Pour the dressing over the prawn mixture and toss gently to coat everything.

6 Line a salad bowl with lettuce leaves and spoon in the prawn mixture. Serve with lemon wedges to squeeze over the salad.

If you cannot get uncooked freshwater prawns, you can thaw 8oz (225g) frozen cooked peeled prawns to mix into the salad, but these will have a higher salt content.

Young spinach leaves make a simple and colourful foil for plump and tender Dublin Bay prawns, sharpened with a wine and lemon dressing. Smaller freshwater prawns (far right) partner fetta cheese and grilled red pepper on a bed of frilled lettuce leaves flavoured with dill and spring onion.

Prawn and spinach salad

SERVES 4
PREPARATION TIME: 15 minutes

ONE SERVING

CALORIES 140

TOTAL FAT 5g

SATURATED FAT 1g

CARBOHYDRATES 2g

ADDED SUGAR 0

FIBRE 2g

SODIUM 315mg

16 large uncooked freshwater prawns, shelled and
de-veined
1lb (450g) young spinach leaves, trimmed
and washed
2 tablespoons lemon juice
2 tablespoons dry white wine
Freshly ground black pepper
1 tablespoon virgin olive oil

1 Boil the prawns for 2-3 minutes in unsalted
water. Rinse with cold water, drain and pat dry.

2 Dry the spinach leaves gently but thoroughly
with kitchen paper or a clean cloth. Tear
the leaves into small pieces put them in a salad
bowl and mix in the prawns.

3 Pour the lemon juice and white wine into
a bowl, season with pepper and whisk in the oil.
Pour the dressing over the salad and serve.

Rice, orange and walnut salad

SERVES 4
PREPARATION TIME: 15 minutes
COOKING TIME: 35 minutes

8oz (225g) brown rice
2 large oranges, gently scrubbed under warm water
1 tablespoon cider vinegar
1 level teaspoon Dijon mustard
1 tablespoon walnut oil
1 tablespoon virgin olive oil
1 level tablespoon chopped fresh chervil
1 level tablespoon chopped fresh tarragon
Freshly ground black pepper
5 spring onions, trimmed and chopped
3oz (85g) walnuts, chopped
4oz (115g) small strawberries, hulled and cut in half
Chervil sprigs to garnish

ONE SERVING	
CALORIES	415
TOTAL FAT	20g
SATURATED FAT	2g
CARBOHYDRATES	55g
ADDED SUGAR	0
FIBRE	3g
SODIUM	70mg

1 Cook the rice

2 Finely grate the rind from one orange into a large bowl. Stir in the vinegar, mustard, walnut oil, olive oil, chopped chervil and tarragon. Season with the pepper, then mix in the rice and spring onions. Cover and leave until cold.

3 Peel and segment the oranges, and cut each segment into four, discarding any pips. Stir the oranges, walnuts and strawberries into the rice. Turn the salad into a serving bowl and garnish with the chervil sprigs.

You can use 3 clementines in place of the oranges. Add the grated rind of 2 clementines to the dressing, and cut the segments in half. Use wild strawberries when they are in season.

Spinach and bacon salad

ONE SERVING	
CALORIES	85
TOTAL FAT	4g
SATURATED FAT	1g
CARBOHYDRATES	5g
ADDED SUGAR	0
FIBRE	3g
SODIUM	280mg

SERVES 4
PREPARATION TIME: 10 minutes
COOKING TIME: 10 minutes

1lb (450g) fresh young spinach leaves, trimmed and washed
1 lean rasher unsmoked back bacon
2 teaspoons olive oil
1 medium red or yellow pepper, de-seeded and cut into strips
1 small red onion, peeled and finely chopped
1 clove garlic, peeled and finely chopped
4 tablespoons dry white wine
4 tablespoons cider vinegar
Freshly ground black pepper

1 Dry the spinach gently but thoroughly with kitchen paper or a clean cloth. Tear the leaves into small pieces and spread them in a large heatproof serving bowl.

2 Grill the bacon under a moderate heat for 5-6 minutes, or until crisp. Drain it on kitchen paper and set aside.

3 Heat the oil in a small saucepan and cook the pepper strips, onion and garlic in it over a moderate heat, stirring, for 2 minutes. Pour in the wine and vinegar, and season with black pepper. Bring to the boil, then reduce the heat and simmer, uncovered, for 1 minute. Pour the dressing over the spinach while still hot, and toss well.

4 Trim all the fat off the bacon. Cut the meat into fine strips, scatter them over the spinach and serve the salad at once.

To vary the taste of the salad, you can use crisp lettuce leaves or lamb's lettuce to replace all the spinach, or part of it.

Chopped walnuts add crunch and a rich flavour to a brown rice and orange salad (top), while strawberries give a fragrant and unusual touch, as well as extra juiciness. Bacon makes a delicious savoury contrast with peppery young spinach leaves just wilting to a delicious tenderness in a hot and sharp dressing.

Roasted vegetable salad

ONE SERVING

CALORIES 125

TOTAL FAT 8g

SATURATED FAT 1g

CARBOHYDRATES 11g

ADDED SUGAR 0

FIBRE 3g

SODIUM 10mg

Roasting the peppers intensifies their flavour, and garlic, herbs and citrus juice heighten the savoury appeal of this unusual salad.

SERVES 4
PREPARATION TIME: 15 minutes, plus 1 hour to cool
COOKING TIME: 30 minutes
OVEN: Preheat to 200°C (400°F, gas mark 6)

1 whole bulb garlic
3 medium peppers, red, green and yellow, de-seeded and sliced lengthways into strips
1 large onion, peeled and thickly sliced
2 tablespoons virgin olive oil
1 level teaspoon dried oregano
1/2 level teaspoon ground cumin
Freshly ground black pepper
1 large tomato, de-seeded and cut into squares
1 tablespoon lime or lemon juice
2 level tablespoons chopped fresh parsley or basil

1 Separate the garlic bulb into individual cloves and peel each clove. Put the garlic, red, green and yellow peppers, onion, oil, oregano and cumin in a large ovenproof dish. Season with black pepper, and stir gently to coat the vegetables with the oil.

2 Cook the vegetables in the heated oven, uncovered, for 15 minutes, stirring them occasionally. Mix in the tomato and cook for a further 15 minutes, stirring two or three times to prevent sticking at the bottom.

3 Spoon the vegetables into a serving dish, stir in the lime or lemon juice, and leave until cold. Sprinkle the chopped parsley or basil over the salad just before serving.

> **TIP**
> *To enjoy the full character of this dish, use the whole bulb of garlic without hesitation. Roasted garlic has a mild, nutty taste quite different from that of raw garlic.*

Waldorf salad

ONE SERVING

CALORIES 155

TOTAL FAT 9g

SATURATED FAT 1g

CARBOHYDRATES 17g

ADDED SUGAR 0

FIBRE 2g

SODIUM 100mg

SERVES 4
PREPARATION TIME: 20 minutes

3 medium dessert apples, cored and cut into chunks
6oz (175g) seedless green grapes
2 sticks celery, trimmed and finely sliced
2 spring onions, trimmed and finely chopped
1 tablespoon virgin olive oil

1 level teaspoon Dijon mustard
1 tablespoon lemon juice
1/4 teaspoon celery seeds
Freshly ground black pepper
12 large radicchio leaves, washed and dried
2 bunches watercress, washed, thick stems removed
2 level tablespoons chopped walnuts
Sage sprigs to garnish

TIP
To make watercress crisp, rinse it under a cold tap, shake and put into a polythene bag. Tie the top and keep the bag in the bottom of the refrigerator. Use within 48 hours.

1 Mix the apples with the grapes, celery and spring onions.

2 Whisk the oil with the mustard, lemon juice and celery seeds until the mixture thickens slightly. Season with pepper, pour over the apple mixture and toss gently.

3 Arrange the radicchio leaves in cup shapes on a serving plate or in individual salad bowls.

Half fill with the watercress and spoon on the apple mixture. Sprinkle the walnuts on top and garnish with sage.

Crisp apples such as Granny Smiths or Sturmers give this salad a pleasing variety of textures, and if you can get purple sage it will complement the radicchio's colour. For a creamier dressing, use Greek yoghurt in place of the olive oil.

This variation of the salad first created at New York's Waldorf-Astoria hotel, uses grapes to sweeten and spring onions to sharpen the usual blend of apple, celery and walnuts. A mustard and lemon dressing replaces the mayonnaise, adding piquancy and reducing calories. Radicchio leaves make the glowing salad bowls.

PASTA AND GRAINS

Substantial helpings of starchy food teamed with quite small amounts of protein are a winning combination with nutritionists as well as with families. Here are your favourite pasta recipes and risottos, carefully pruned of fat, and some more unusual dishes that will soon become favourites. Often quick to make and inexpensive, many of these recipes originated in countries fringing the Mediterranean, where the diets are among the healthiest in the world.

Cannelloni with chicken and walnuts

ONE SERVING

CALORIES 465

TOTAL FAT 23g

SATURATED FAT 5g

CARBOHYDRATES 39g

ADDED SUGAR 0

FIBRE 2g

SODIUM 410mg

TIP
*An easy way
to put the chicken
filling into the
cannelloni tubes is
to use a piping bag
fitted with a large
plain nozzle.*

SERVES 4
PREPARATION TIME: 20 minutes
COOKING TIME: 35 minutes
OVEN: Preheat to 180°C (350°F, gas mark 4)

2oz (60g) shelled walnuts, finely chopped
*6oz (175g) cooked chicken without skin or bone,
minced or finely chopped*
¼ level teaspoon ground mace
4oz (115g) ricotta cheese
4oz (115g) cottage cheese
12 tubes ready-to-use cannelloni
1oz (30g) polyunsaturated margarine
1oz (30g) plain flour
Freshly ground black pepper
¾ pint (425ml) skimmed milk
Bay leaf
14oz (400g) tinned chopped tomatoes
1oz (30g) grated reduced-fat Cheddar cheese

1 Reserve 1 tablespoon of walnuts. Mix the rest with the chicken, mace, ricotta and cottage cheese. Fill the cannelloni with the mixture.

2 Melt the margarine in a saucepan, stir in the flour, season with pepper, and cook gently for 1 minute. Gradually mix in the milk, put in the bay leaf and bring to the boil, stirring until the sauce thickens. Discard the bay leaf.

3 Spread the tomatoes in a large gratin dish and lay the cannelloni in one layer on top. Cover with the sauce and scatter on the Cheddar and reserved walnuts. Cook in the heated oven, covered, for 15 minutes, then uncover and cook for 20 minutes more, or until browned on top.

Garnish the cannelloni with parsley, and serve with colourful side salads or steamed broccoli.

*A delicately flavoured
mixture of chicken and
soft cheese fills the
pasta tubes, which cook
in béchamel sauce and
juicy tomatoes.*

Cannelloni with ricotta and spinach

ONE SERVING

CALORIES 470

TOTAL FAT 18g

SATURATED FAT 6g

CARBOHYDRATES 57g

ADDED SUGAR 0

FIBRE 5g

SODIUM 455mg

SERVES 4
PREPARATION TIME: 35 minutes
COOKING TIME: 30 minutes
OVEN: Preheat to 180°C (350°F, gas mark 4)

1 tablespoon olive oil
1 large onion, peeled and chopped

2 cloves garlic, peeled and chopped
1 level tablespoon chopped fresh basil
½ level teaspoon dried marjoram
Freshly ground black pepper
14oz (400g) tinned peeled tomatoes
1 tablespoon tomato purée
9oz (250g) fresh spinach, washed and trimmed

3oz (85g) ricotta or curd cheese
4oz (115g) cottage cheese
½ level teaspoon freshly grated nutmeg
8 large sheets lasagne
1oz (30g) grated Parmesan cheese

1 Heat the oil in a frying pan and cook the onion and half the garlic in it over a moderate heat for about 5 minutes. Stir in the basil and marjoram and season with pepper. Take out and set aside 2 tablespoons of the mixture.

2 Stir the tomatoes, their juice and the tomato purée into the pan of onion mixture and cook over a moderate heat for 20 minutes, stirring occasionally to break down the tomatoes.

3 In the meantime, prepare the filling. Blanch the spinach in unsalted boiling water for 30 seconds, pour it into a colander and rinse it with cold water. Squeeze the spinach hard, then turn it into a bowl, chop it roughly and work in the ricotta or curd cheese, cottage cheese, remaining garlic, reserved onion mixture and nutmeg, and season with pepper.

4 Cook the lasagne for 2-3 minutes, then rinse it with cold water and drain well. Lay the sheets on a board and spread some filling across a narrow end of each sheet, dividing the mixture equally between them. Roll the sheets up to form cannelloni.

5 Pour half the tomato sauce into a baking dish and lay the cannelloni on top, seam side down. Pour the remaining sauce over them.

6 Cover the dish and cook in the heated oven for 25 minutes, then uncover, sprinkle with the Parmesan and cook for 5 minutes more to brown lightly before serving.

The astringent flavour of spinach combines well with mild soft cheese to make a creamy filling for rolls of fresh pasta. A tomato sauce tangy with herbs makes a pleasingly sharp contrast in taste and colour.

Pasta salad with salmon and spinach

ONE SERVING

CALORIES 375

TOTAL FAT 14g

SATURATED FAT 3g

CARBOHYDRATES 43g

ADDED SUGAR 0

FIBRE 3g

SODIUM 265mg

TIP
Use only fresh, young and tender spinach leaves as they have the sweetest flavour. The bitterness of larger leaves would dominate the flavour of the salmon.

SERVES 4
PREPARATION TIME: 25 minutes
COOKING TIME: 10 minutes

7oz (200g) fusilli
2 pints (1.15 litres) water
1 small onion, peeled and chopped
½ lemon, quartered
1 sprig parsley
10oz (275g) salmon steaks
1 clove garlic, peeled and crushed
1 level tablespoon snipped chives
½ level teaspoon fennel seeds, crushed
4oz (115g) low-fat natural yoghurt
1 tablespoon virgin olive oil
½ level teaspoon paprika
7oz (200g) tender young spinach leaves, washed, patted dry and finely shredded
1 medium courgette, trimmed and thinly sliced

1 Cook the fusilli, rinse with cold water and drain well.

2 Pour the water into a large frying pan with the onion, lemon and parsley. Bring to a simmer then put in the salmon and poach gently for about 5 minutes, or until the fish flakes easily and is opaque all through. Lift the salmon out of the pan, remove the skin and bones and flake the flesh coarsely. Leave to cool for 15 minutes.

3 Meanwhile, combine the garlic, chives, fennel seeds, yoghurt, oil and paprika in a salad bowl.

4 Mix the pasta with the spinach and courgette. Gently fold in the cold salmon, top with the yoghurt dressing and serve.

Lightly poached salmon makes an elegant contrast to crunchy courgette and tender young spinach. Spirals of pasta add body to this eye-catching salad, topped with a creamy yoghurt, chive and fennel dressing.

Pasta shells are the heart of this simple salad, which is flavoured with red onion and black olives and piled on a lacy base of frisée leaves.

Summer pasta salad

ONE SERVING

CALORIES 210

TOTAL FAT 5g

SATURATED FAT 1g

CARBOHYDRATES 37g

ADDED SUGAR 0

FIBRE 3g

SODIUM 175mg

SERVES 4
PREPARATION TIME: 15 minutes

6oz (175g) miniature pasta shells or macaroni
1 tablespoon virgin olive oil
4 level tablespoons chopped fresh basil or parsley
1 small red onion, peeled and finely chopped
Freshly ground black pepper
½ medium cucumber, cut into cubes
1 large beef tomato, skinned, de-seeded and chopped
4 black olives, stoned and thinly sliced
Small frisée lettuce, washed and dried

1 Cook the pasta, rinse with cold water and drain well.

2 Combine the oil, basil or parsley and onion in a salad bowl, and season with pepper. Stir in the pasta until lightly coated.

3 Stir the cucumber and tomato into the pasta mixture and scatter on the olives.

4 Line four individual salad plates with the lettuce leaves and spoon a share of the pasta mixture onto each one.

Farfalle with broccoli and nuts

SERVES 4
PREPARATION TIME: 15 minutes
COOKING TIME: 30 minutes

14oz (400g) broccoli, trimmed and divided
into florets
1 tablespoon olive oil
2 cloves garlic, peeled and finely chopped
2lb (900g) ripe tomatoes, peeled, de-seeded
and chopped
2 level tablespoons seedless sultanas, chopped
¼ level teaspoon cayenne pepper
2oz (60g) pine nuts or chopped blanched almonds
3 level tablespoons chopped fresh parsley
10oz (275g) farfalle
1oz (30g) grated Parmesan cheese

1 Simmer the broccoli in a little unsalted
water in a covered saucepan for 4-5 minutes,
until just beginning to soften. Rinse with
cold water and drain.

2 Heat the oil in a large frying pan and cook
the garlic in it over a moderate heat for about
2 minutes, or until golden. Stir in the tomatoes,
sultanas and cayenne pepper and cook,
uncovered, for 15 minutes. Add the nuts and
parsley and cook for a further 5 minutes.

3 Meanwhile, cook the farfalle
drain and spread in a warmed serving dish.

4 Stir the broccoli into the tomato sauce and
heat through for 2-3 minutes. Pour the sauce
over the farfalle and sprinkle with the Parmesan
just before serving.

A crunchy side salad of celeriac in a lemon
dressing balances the sweet tomato sauce.

*This attractive dish with its tightly budded broccoli
florets and butterfly pasta is a rich source of fibre.*

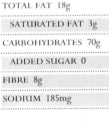

ONE SERVING	
CALORIES	505
TOTAL FAT	18g
SATURATED FAT	3g
CARBOHYDRATES	70g
ADDED SUGAR	0
FIBRE	8g
SODIUM	185mg

Fusilli with bacon and mushrooms

SERVES 4
PREPARATION TIME: 10 minutes
COOKING TIME: 15 minutes

2oz (60g) grated Parmesan cheese
2 tablespoons freshly chopped parsley
6oz (175g) Greek yoghurt
Freshly ground black pepper
1 tablespoon olive oil
4oz (115g) unsmoked back bacon with
fat removed, cut into thin strips
6oz (175g) mushrooms, wiped and thinly sliced
1 medium onion, peeled and chopped
2 cloves garlic, peeled and finely chopped
10oz (275g) fusilli
4 tablespoons dry white wine
Chopped fresh parsley or basil to garnish

1 Mix the Parmesan and parsley into the yoghurt and season with pepper. Cover and put in the refrigerator.

2 Heat the oil in a small saucepan and toss the bacon in it over a moderate heat for 2-3 minutes until lightly browned. Add the mushrooms, onion and garlic and cook, stirring occasionally, for about 5 minutes, or until the onion softens.

3 Meanwhile, cook the fusilli

4 Pour the wine onto the bacon and mushrooms and cook for 2-3 minutes, or until it has almost evaporated. Stir in the yoghurt mixture and reheat the sauce without boiling.

5 When the fusilli are cooked 'al dente', drain and spread on a warmed serving dish. Pour on the sauce and garnish with the parsley or basil.

A dish of sweet fresh garden peas or a crisp fennel and cabbage salad would give a pleasing contrast to the flavours of the pasta sauce.

ONE SERVING

CALORIES 450

TOTAL FAT 15g

SATURATED FAT 6g

CARBOHYDRATES 58g

ADDED SUGAR 0

FIBRE 3g

SODIUM 810mg

TIP
It is quicker to snip parsley than to chop it. Bunch the parsley sprigs together, hold them near the tips and snip them finely with kitchen scissors, gradually moving your grip down the stems as you snip.

The creamy bacon and mushroom sauce with its added tang of wine is easy to make, and turns the pasta spirals called fusilli into a satisfyingly savoury dish.

Vegetable lasagne

SERVES 4
PREPARATION TIME: 45 minutes
COOKING TIME: 35 minutes
OVEN: Preheat to 200°C (400°F, gas mark 6)

2 bulbs garlic
2 tablespoons olive oil
1 small onion, peeled and chopped
9oz (250g) courgettes, trimmed and diced
9oz (250g) mushrooms, wiped and finely sliced
5oz (150g) shelled fresh peas or frozen peas
2 teaspoons lemon juice
¼ level teaspoon cayenne pepper
Freshly ground black pepper
2½ level tablespoons plain flour
½ pint (285ml) skimmed milk
½ level teaspoon dried oregano
2oz (60g) grated Parmesan cheese
16 small sheets homemade green lasagne

ONE SERVING	
CALORIES 545	
TOTAL FAT 22g	
SATURATED FAT 6g	
CARBOHYDRATES 71g	
ADDED SUGAR 0	
FIBRE 6g	
SODIUM 315mg	

1 Wrap the two whole unpeeled garlic bulbs separately in foil and cook them in the heated oven for 20 minutes. Remove and leave to cool, then separate the cloves and peel them. Mash them in a bowl with a fork and set aside.

2 Heat half the oil in a saucepan and cook the onion and courgettes in it over a moderate heat for about 5 minutes. Stir in the mushrooms and cook for 3 minutes, then the peas and cook for 1 more minute. Sprinkle in the lemon juice and cayenne pepper, and season lightly with black pepper. Remove from the heat.

3 Heat the remaining oil in a small saucepan, stir in the flour and cook gently for 1 minute. Gradually stir in the milk, bring to the boil, stirring, then simmer for 3 minutes. Mix in the oregano, Parmesan and garlic. Mix all but about 6 tablespoons of the sauce into the vegetables.

4 Cook the lasagne for 2-3 minutes and drain. Cover the bottom of a lightly oiled ovenproof dish with a third of the lasagne. Spread on half the vegetable mixture. Repeat with another layer of lasagne and vegetables, then top with the remaining lasagne. Spread the reserved sauce on top.

5 Cover the dish and cook in the heated oven for 20 minutes. Uncover and cook for a further 15 minutes, until browned on top.

Serve a salad of radicchio and red onion with the dish. You can use dried lasagne instead of fresh but it will need a third more sauce.

The generous amount of garlic used in the sauce does not give an extravagantly garlicky flavour, but serves to intensify the taste of the vegetables in this variation on a filling pasta favourite.

Linguine with peas and tuna

SERVES 4
PREPARATION TIME: 5 minutes
COOKING TIME: 20 minutes

10oz (275g) linguine
1 tablespoon olive oil

1 level tablespoon plain flour
½ pint (285ml) skimmed milk
7oz (200g) frozen peas
7oz (200g) tinned tuna in oil, drained and flaked
2oz (60g) grated Parmesan cheese
Freshly ground black pepper

Sweet green peas and meaty tuna in a light sauce mingle with thin strips of pasta, which have the best texture when they are newly made.

ONE SERVING
CALORIES 560
TOTAL FAT 23g
SATURATED FAT 6g
CARBOHYDRATES 58g
ADDED SUGAR 0
FIBRE 5g
SODIUM 455mg

1 Heat the oil in a large saucepan, mix in the flour and gradually stir in the milk. Bring to the boil over a moderate heat, stirring all the time, then reduce the heat and continue cooking for 2 minutes, until the sauce thickens slightly.

2 Add the peas to the sauce and cook for 4 minutes. Mix in the tuna and Parmesan and season with pepper. Heat through gently, without boiling, for about 5 minutes.

3 Meanwhile, cook the linguine for 2-3 minutes and drain well.

Serve the linguine in heated bowls. Side salads of grated carrots give a crisp finishing touch.

41

Linguine and tomato pie

ONE SERVING

CALORIES 385

TOTAL FAT 13g

SATURATED FAT 5g

CARBOHYDRATES 50g

ADDED SUGAR 0

FIBRE 4g

SODIUM 300mg

SERVES 4
PREPARATION TIME: 20 minutes
COOKING TIME: 35 minutes
OVEN: Preheat to 190°C (375°F, gas mark 5)

1 tablespoon olive oil
8oz (225g) linguine
1 medium onion, peeled and finely chopped
3 cloves garlic, peeled and finely chopped

2 level tablespoons chopped fresh parsley
1½ level teaspoons dried oregano
1 level teaspoon dried basil
1 tablespoon lemon juice
Freshly ground black pepper
3oz (85g) ricotta or curd cheese
1 egg, size 2, beaten
1lb (450g) tomatoes, skinned and sliced
3oz (85g) grated low-fat Cheddar cheese
½ oz (15g) grated Parmesan cheese

1 Grease a loose-bottomed or hinged-side cake tin 8in (20cm) in diameter with a little oil.

2 Cook the linguine and drain well.

3 Meanwhile, heat the rest of the oil in a heavy-based saucepan and fry the onion and garlic in it over a moderate heat for about 5 minutes. Mix in the linguine, scatter on the parsley, oregano and basil, sprinkle with the lemon juice, season with pepper and toss well.

4 Combine the ricotta or curd cheese and the egg with the linguine. Spoon half the mixture into the prepared tin and press it down lightly.

5 Arrange half the tomato slices on top and scatter half the Cheddar over them. Spoon the remaining pasta mixture on top and press down lightly. Cover with the rest of the tomatoes and Cheddar and sprinkle with the Parmesan.

6 Cover and bake in the heated oven for 30 minutes, then uncover and bake for a further 5 minutes, or until browned on top.

7 Leave the pie to cool for 10 minutes, then run a knife round the edge to loosen it from the tin. Remove the side of the tin and slide the pie onto a warmed serving plate.

Tomato layers and herbs moisten and flavour an original treat – narrow ribbons of tender pasta bound with egg to make an unusual cheese-topped pie.

Macaroni with leeks and tarragon

ONE SERVING
....
CALORIES 475
....
TOTAL FAT 17g
....
SATURATED FAT 9g
....
CARBOHYDRATES 60g
....
ADDED SUGAR 0
....
FIBRE 5g
....
SODIUM 385mg
....

TIP
*Always add
mustard as near as
possible to the end
of cooking, because
its flavour is
lessened
by cooking.*

SERVES 4
PREPARATION TIME: 25 minutes
COOKING TIME: 25 minutes
OVEN: Preheat to 200°C (400°F, gas mark 6)

7oz (200g) macaroni or macaroni spirals
½ oz (15g) slightly salted butter
3 medium leeks, trimmed, finely sliced and washed
3 level tablespoons plain flour
1¼ pints (725ml) skimmed milk
Freshly ground black pepper
2 level tablespoons chopped fresh tarragon
1 level teaspoon English mustard powder
4oz (115g) grated mature Cheddar cheese
1 level tablespoon wholemeal breadcrumbs
1½ level tablespoons sesame seeds
Tomato slices and sprigs of fresh tarragon to garnish

1 Cook the macaroni and drain
it thoroughly.

2 Meanwhile, melt the butter in a saucepan
and gently cook the leeks in it, covered, for
3 minutes. Mix in the flour, cook for 1 minute,
then gradually stir in the milk. Bring the sauce
slowly to the boil, stirring continuously.

3 Season with pepper, mix in the tarragon and
simmer for about 5 minutes. Mix the mustard
with a little of the sauce, then stir it back into
the pan. Fold in the Cheddar and macaroni.

4 Pour the mixture into a deep ovenproof
dish. Mix the breadcrumbs and sesame seeds
and scatter them over the macaroni. Bake in
the heated oven for about 25 minutes, until
bubbling and lightly browned on top. Garnish
with the tomato slices and tarragon sprigs.

A crisp salad of frisée and lamb's lettuce makes
a refreshing accompaniment.

Traditional macaroni cheese is given an appetising new edge with leeks, tarragon and a crisp sesame topping.

Ham, pea and noodle gratin

SERVES 4
PREPARATION TIME: 10 minutes
COOKING TIME: 20 minutes

ONE SERVING

CALORIES 465

TOTAL FAT 7g

SATURATED FAT 3g

CARBOHYDRATES 80g

ADDED SUGAR 0

FIBRE 6g

SODIUM 795mg

10oz (275g) Italian noodles or tagliatelle
½ oz (15g) slightly salted butter
2 level tablespoons plain flour
¼ level teaspoon dried sage
¼ level teaspoon dried marjoram
½ level teaspoon dried thyme
⅛ level teaspoon ground mace

¾ pint (425ml) skimmed milk
Freshly ground black pepper
6oz (175g) cooked ham with fat removed, diced
8oz (225g) cooked peas
3 tomatoes, sliced
1½ oz (45g) fresh fine white breadcrumbs

1 Cook the noodles and drain.

2 Meanwhile, melt the butter in a saucepan and stir in the flour, sage, marjoram, thyme and mace. Cook over a gentle heat for 1 minute, then gradually stir in the milk. Bring to the boil, stirring continuously, until the sauce thickens slightly. Season with pepper, then mix in the ham and peas, and simmer for 2 minutes to heat thoroughly.

3 Mix the pasta in until it is coated with the sauce, then turn everything into a heatproof serving dish. Arrange the sliced tomatoes on top and sprinkle with the breadcrumbs.

4 Put the gratin under a hot grill for about 3 minutes, until browned on top.

A green salad or a cucumber and fruit salad goes well with this dish. For a change of flavour you can use cooked prawns or smoked haddock in place of the ham.

Savoury ham and sweet green peas are combined with a herb sauce in this simple dish of Italian noodles which is finished with a crisp, bright topping.

Chinese noodles with nuts and apricots

SERVES 4
PREPARATION TIME: 15 minutes
COOKING TIME: 20 minutes

ONE SERVING

CALORIES 640

TOTAL FAT 27g

SATURATED FAT 6g

CARBOHYDRATES 92g

ADDED SUGAR 0

FIBRE 7g

SODIUM 435mg

12oz (340g) Chinese medium egg noodles
2 tablespoons sesame oil
2 level teaspoons peeled and chopped root ginger
1 clove garlic, peeled and finely chopped
1 small onion, peeled and finely chopped
1 medium carrot, peeled and cut into fine strips

1 stick celery, trimmed and cut into fine strips
4oz (115g) ready-to-use dried apricots, chopped
2oz (60g) unsalted shelled peanuts,
lightly toasted and skinned
2oz (60g) unsalted cashew nuts
4oz (115g) silken tofu, diced
1 tablespoon soy sauce
1 tablespoon hoisin sauce
1 tablespoon dry sherry
4oz (115g) fresh bean sprouts

The crunchy texture of this unmistakably Chinese dish is elegantly balanced by the soft, tangy apricots. Rich brown hoisin sauce adds its spicy sweetness, while the dry sherry is a substitute for the authentic rice wine.

1 Cook the noodles in unsalted water and drain.

2 Heat the oil in a large wok or frying pan and toss the ginger, garlic and onion in it over a high heat for 2-3 minutes. Stir in the carrot and celery and toss for 2 minutes more.

3 Mix in the apricots, peanuts, cashew nuts and tofu and cook gently for 2 minutes, stirring

frequently, before pouring in the soy sauce, hoisin sauce and sherry.

4 Add the noodles and bean sprouts and toss together until the ingredients are well mixed. Cook over a moderate heat for 2-3 minutes, until everything is piping hot.

Serve the noodles at once in warmed individual bowls with side salads of cos-type lettuce.

TIP
When the peanuts are toasted, fold them a few at a time in kitchen paper and rub briskly between your palms to take off the brown skins, which tend to stick in the throat if left in the dish.

Penne with spinach and cheese

SERVES 4
PREPARATION TIME: 20 minutes
COOKING TIME: 15 minutes

9oz (250g) penne
1 tablespoon olive oil
1 small onion, peeled and chopped
2 cloves garlic, peeled and finely chopped

1lb (450g) fresh spinach, trimmed, well washed
and torn into shreds
4fl oz (115ml) skimmed milk
4fl oz (115ml) vegetable or chicken stock
(see p.19)
1½ oz (45g) grated Parmesan cheese
4oz (115g) cottage cheese
Freshly ground black pepper

The astringent spinach harmonises well with the slightly smoky Parmesan in creating a delicious light sauce to coat the quill-shaped pasta.

ONE SERVING	
CALORIES	365
TOTAL FAT	9g
SATURATED FAT	3g
CARBOHYDRATES	55g
ADDED SUGAR	0
FIBRE	5g
SODIUM	480mg

1 Cook the penne and drain.

2 Meanwhile, heat the oil in a large saucepan and cook the onion and garlic in it over a moderate heat for 5 minutes, until the onion softens. Stir in the spinach, milk, stock, Parmesan and cottage cheese, and season with pepper. Bring to the boil, stirring, and simmer for about 3 minutes, until the sauce thickens.

3 Turn the penne into the spinach sauce and mix well until the pasta is coated before serving onto warmed plates.

A tomato salad sprinkled with chives makes a colourful side dish. When fresh spinach is not available, you can use 8oz (225g) frozen leaf spinach, completely thawed and drained well before being added to the sauce.

Pasta shells with chickpeas

ONE SERVING
....
CALORIES 335
....
TOTAL FAT 7g
....
SATURATED FAT 1g
....
CARBOHYDRATES 61g
....
ADDED SUGAR 0
....
FIBRE 10g
....
SODIUM 195mg

Leek, olives and a generous amount of herbs enliven this simple dish, which combines wholemeal pasta and chickpeas, providing an excellent source of fibre.

SERVES 4
PREPARATION TIME: 10 minutes
COOKING TIME: 15 minutes

10oz (275g) wholemeal pasta shells
1 tablespoon olive oil
1 small leek, trimmed, thinly sliced and washed
1 small onion, peeled and finely chopped
4 fresh sage leaves, chopped, or ½ level teaspoon dried sage
1 small sprig fresh rosemary, or ½ level teaspoon dried rosemary
2 large ripe tomatoes, chopped
8oz (225g) cooked chickpeas (see p.17) with 3 tablespoons of their cooking liquid
1 level tablespoon dried oregano
Freshly ground black pepper
6 green olives, stoned and chopped
Shredded fresh lovage or celery leaves

1 Cook the pasta shells and drain.

2 Meanwhile, heat the oil in a saucepan and cook the leek and onion in it over a high heat for 2 minutes. Add the sage, rosemary and tomatoes, cover and simmer for 5 minutes.

3 Rub the chickpeas and the reserved cooking liquid through a sieve, or reduce them to a purée in a blender. Stir in the oregano, season with pepper and heat to boiling point.

4 Turn the pasta into a heated serving dish and spoon the vegetables on top, discarding the rosemary sprig. Top with the chickpea purée and garnish with the olives and lovage or celery.

A crisp green salad and some bread are the best accompaniments for this savoury pasta dish.

Stuffed pasta shells and watercress sauce

SERVES 4
PREPARATION TIME: 40 minutes
COOKING TIME: 15 minutes
OVEN: Preheat to 220°C (425°F, gas mark 7)

ONE SERVING

CALORIES 210

TOTAL FAT 8g

SATURATED FAT 2g

CARBOHYDRATES 22g

ADDED SUGAR 0

FIBRE 4g

SODIUM 105mg

1 tablespoon olive oil
8oz (225g) button mushrooms, wiped and chopped
1 medium onion, peeled and finely chopped
6oz (175g) courgettes, trimmed and chopped
6oz (175g) red pepper, de-seeded and chopped
4oz (115g) chicken breast without skin or bone, finely chopped
½ oz (15g) wholemeal breadcrumbs
2 level teaspoons dried mixed herbs
Freshly ground black pepper
3 tablespoons chicken stock
16 large pasta shells, about 2¼ in (55mm) long

For the watercress sauce:
6fl oz (175ml) chicken stock
6oz (175g) watercress, trimmed and washed
5oz (150g) fromage frais

1 Heat the oil in a frying pan and cook the mushrooms, onion, courgettes and red pepper in it over a moderate heat for 10 minutes, until softened, stirring from time to time.

2 Mix in the chicken and stir over a moderate heat for 5 minutes or until cooked through. Sprinkle in the breadcrumbs and herbs, season with black pepper and moisten with the stock. Bring to the boil, then set aside.

3 Cook the pasta shells and drain.

4 Meanwhile, to prepare the watercress sauce, boil the stock rapidly in a saucepan until reduced by half, then stir in the watercress and boil for 1 minute. Cool slightly before blending with the fromage frais in a food processor.

5 Fill the pasta shells with the mushroom mixture and arrange them in one layer in a baking dish. Pour the watercress sauce round them, cover the dish and cook in the heated oven for 15 minutes or until bubbling hot.

A tomato salad and lightly toasted bread with a little olive oil and basil to sprinkle on add extra Italian touches to the pasta.

Pasta shells with sardines and pesto

SERVES 4
PREPARATION TIME: 20 minutes
COOKING TIME: 25 minutes

2 large red peppers, halved and de-seeded
2 beef tomatoes, peeled and chopped
1 tablespoon tomato purée
1 clove garlic, peeled and crushed
4 level tablespoons pesto sauce
12oz (340g) pasta shells
4 fresh sardines, each about 4oz (115g), with heads removed, scaled, cleaned, gutted and boned
8 black olives, stoned and quartered
1oz (30g) pine nuts
1 level tablespoon chopped fresh oregano leaves

1 Grill the red peppers, skin side up, until the skin blisters. Leave to cool in a covered bowl, then peel off the skin and chop the flesh.

2 Use a food mill or food processor to blend the pepper, tomatoes, tomato purée, garlic and pesto. Pour the sauce into a frying pan and simmer, uncovered, for 10 minutes or until slightly reduced and thickened.

3 Meanwhile, cook the pasta shells.

4 Lay the sardines in the sauce and cook over a gentle heat for 10 minutes.

5 Turn the drained pasta shells onto warmed plates and arrange the sardines on top. Stir the olives into the sauce, then pour it over the fish. Scatter with the pine nuts and oregano immediately before serving.

A salad of lamb's lettuce gives a touch of sharpness to contrast with the rich fish sauce.

ONE SERVING	
CALORIES	545
TOTAL FAT	19g
SATURATED FAT	2g
CARBOHYDRATES	72g
ADDED SUGAR	0
FIBRE	5g
SODIUM	555mg

> **TIP**
> *When you cannot get fresh sardines, you can use sardines tinned in oil, but drain them well and press them lightly with kitchen paper to absorb as much oil as you can.*

Pesto, a classic Italian partner for pasta, lends some of its peppery taste to the sauce, and penetrates the delicate sardines. Pine nuts and olives reinforce the Mediterranean flavours.

Spaghetti with prawns and capers

SERVES 4
PREPARATION TIME: 5 minutes
COOKING TIME: 20 minutes

1 tablespoon olive oil
1 clove garlic, peeled and finely chopped

14oz (400g) tinned peeled tomatoes
1 level teaspoon dried basil
9oz (250g) spaghetti
5oz (150g) frozen peeled prawns
2 level tablespoons capers, rinsed, dried and chopped
2 level tablespoons chopped fresh marjoram

Capers add their sharp tang to the sweetness of the tomato sauce, giving it a flavour strong enough to complement the savoury prawns.

ONE SERVING

CALORIES 305

TOTAL FAT 5g

SATURATED FAT 1g

CARBOHYDRATES 50g

ADDED SUGAR 0

FIBRE 3g

SODIUM 765mg

1 Heat the oil in a frying pan and toss the garlic in it over a high heat for 30 seconds to flavour the oil. Pour in the tomatoes, stir in the basil and bring to the boil. Reduce the heat and simmer, uncovered, for about 15 minutes to reduce and thicken the sauce. Stir from time to time to break down the tomatoes.

2 Meanwhile, cook the spaghetti and drain well.

3 Stir the prawns and capers into the sauce and heat through for 5 minutes.

4 Turn the spaghetti onto warmed plates. Pour on the sauce and sprinkle with the marjoram just before serving.

Serve the pasta with a side salad of spicy cucumber and red peppers. You can use tinned tuna, drained and flaked, instead of the prawns.

Tagliatelle bolognese

ONE SERVING	
CALORIES	480
TOTAL FAT	10g
SATURATED FAT	3g
CARBOHYDRATES	70g
ADDED SUGAR	0
FIBRE	4g
SODIUM	450mg

SERVES 4
PREPARATION TIME: 15 minutes
COOKING TIME: 40 minutes

1 tablespoon olive oil
1 small onion, peeled and finely chopped
1 clove garlic, peeled and finely chopped
1 medium carrot, peeled and coarsely grated
2oz (60g) mushrooms, wiped and finely chopped

8oz (225g) lean beef, minced
2oz (60g) chicken livers, finely chopped
2oz (60g) Parma ham with fat removed, chopped
1 level teaspoon dried oregano
14oz (400g) tinned tomatoes rubbed through a sieve
Freshly ground black pepper
12oz (340g) tagliatelle
2 level tablespoons fromage frais
Fresh oregano leaves to garnish

1 Heat the oil in a saucepan and cook the onion and garlic in it over a moderate heat for 5 minutes, until soft. Mix in the carrot and mushrooms and cook for 1 minute.

2 Stir in the beef and chicken livers and cook briskly until they lose all traces of pink, breaking up any lumps that form. Mix in the ham, oregano and tomatoes, and season with pepper. Cover and simmer for 25 minutes.

3 Cook the tagliatelle and drain.

4 Turn the tagliatelle into a warmed serving dish and pour the bolognese sauce over it. Top with the fromage frais and oregano leaves.

Serve green beans or a leafy salad with the tagliatelle for a crisp and colourful contrast.

Parma ham and chicken livers give extra flavour to the beef and tomato sauce that is one of Italy's most appreciated exports – and used here on ribbons of pasta.

Armenian bulgur pilau

ONE SERVING	
CALORIES	595
TOTAL FAT	29g
SATURATED FAT	7g
CARBOHYDRATES	55g
ADDED SUGAR	0
FIBRE	6g
SODIUM	165mg

SERVES 4
PREPARATION TIME: 20 minutes
COOKING TIME: 35 minutes

1 tablespoon olive oil
12oz (340g) neck of lamb fillet with fat removed, thinly sliced
1 medium onion, peeled and chopped
1 small green pepper, de-seeded, and cut into small pieces
6oz (175g) medium-ground bulgur wheat
1¼ pints (725ml) vegetable stock

1 large carrot, peeled and finely chopped
2 sticks celery, trimmed and finely chopped
6oz (175g) ready-to-use dried apricots, chopped
1 level teaspoon dried thyme
⅛ level teaspoon salt
Freshly ground black pepper
2 cloves garlic, peeled and crushed
4oz (115g) tahina paste
3fl oz (85ml) water
Strained juice of 1 lemon
Mint sprigs or 2 tablespoons chopped fresh chives to garnish

TIP
After the bulgur wheat has absorbed the stock and become plump, take the pilau off the heat and let it stand in the covered pan for 10 minutes to make the bulgur tender and fluffy.

1 Heat the olive oil in a large saucepan and cook the lamb in it over a moderate heat for about 5 minutes, until lightly browned all over. Lift the meat out of the pan with a slotted spoon and set aside.

2 Cook the onion in the pan over a moderate heat for 5 minutes, until lightly browned. Stir in the green pepper and bulgur wheat and cook for 1 minute. Return the lamb to the pan.

3 Pour in the stock, add the carrot, celery, apricots, thyme and salt, and season with black pepper. Bring to the boil, then turn down the heat, cover and simmer for about 15 minutes, or until the stock is absorbed.

4 Meanwhile, put the garlic and tahina paste in a medium bowl and gradually whisk in the water and the lemon juice, until the mixture has the consistency of whipped cream.

5 Turn the pilau into a warmed serving dish and scatter on the mint sprigs or chives. Serve the tahina sauce separately.

A colourful roasted pepper salad makes a moist, sweet contrast to the pilau.

In some parts of Turkey bulgur wheat, a cracked wheat, replaces rice in the national dish, pilau. This usually contains nuts and fruits and may accompany meat, most often lamb, but here the lamb is cooked in the dish.

Polenta with tomatoes and artichokes

SERVES 4
PREPARATION TIME: 30 minutes
COOKING TIME: 35 minutes

ONE SERVING

CALORIES 395

TOTAL FAT 12g

SATURATED FAT 4g

CARBOHYDRATES 57g

ADDED SUGAR 0

FIBRE 5g

SODIUM 455mg

Artichokes and the maize porridge called polenta are both widely used in Italian cooking. Sun-dried tomatoes and goat's cheese provide further echoes of the Mediterranean in this filling country fare.

1 tablespoon oil from a jar of sun-dried tomatoes
1 large onion, peeled and chopped
2 cloves garlic, peeled and chopped
3oz (85g) sun-dried tomatoes, well drained on kitchen paper and finely chopped
1lb (450g) tomatoes, skinned and chopped
2 courgettes, trimmed and sliced
1 green pepper, de-seeded and chopped
14oz (400g) tinned artichoke hearts, well rinsed, drained and halved
2 pints (1.1 litres) water
8oz (225g) polenta
3½ oz (100g) goat's cheese, crumbled or sliced
Fresh basil leaves to garnish

1 Heat the oil in a large saucepan and fry the onion and garlic in it over a moderate heat for about 5 minutes, until softened.

2 Add the sun-dried tomatoes, fresh tomatoes, courgettes, green pepper and artichoke hearts. Bring the mixture to the boil, then reduce the heat and cover. Simmer for about 30 minutes, stirring from time to time, until the vegetables are tender and the sauce has thickened slightly.

3 Meanwhile, bring the water to the boil in a large saucepan and pour in the polenta in a thin, steady stream, stirring all the time. Keep stirring the polenta over a low heat and, as it thickens, beat it. When the mixture becomes very stiff and begins to pull away from the sides of the pan, spoon it onto a lightly oiled, warmed serving plate. Make a well in the centre and pour in the tomato sauce.

4 Scatter the cheese over the sauce and cook under a hot grill for 4-5 minutes, until the cheese browns lightly. Garnish with the basil.

You can use cornmeal in place of polenta.

Chicken liver risotto

SERVES 4
PREPARATION TIME: 10 minutes, plus 30 minutes
to soak
COOKING TIME: 45 minutes

2 tablespoons olive oil
1 red onion, peeled and thinly sliced
1 clove garlic, peeled and finely chopped
8oz (225g) button mushrooms, wiped and sliced
8oz (225g) fresh chicken livers, rinsed and dried
8oz (225g) arborio or risotto rice
1oz (30g) wild rice, parboiled for 5 minutes
1oz (30g) dried ceps, soaked in hot water
for 30 minutes, drained and roughly chopped
1¾ pints (1 litre) chicken stock
3 level tablespoons chopped fresh parsley
1½ oz (45g) grated Parmesan cheese

1   Heat the oil in a large, heavy-based saucepan
and gently fry the onion, garlic and button
mushrooms in it for about 5 minutes,
until browned. Stir in the
chicken livers and cook
over a moderate heat,
turning to brown
both sides.

2   Pour the arborio or risotto rice and the wild
rice in with the livers and stir in the ceps. Cook
over a low heat, stirring frequently, for about
5 minutes, until the rice is shiny.

3   Pour ¼ pint (150ml) of the stock into the
rice and stir over a low heat until the liquid is
absorbed. Continue to stir in these small
amounts of stock, letting the rice absorb each
addition before adding the next. It will take
about 35 minutes to use all the stock.

4   Stir in the parsley, turn the risotto into a
warm serving dish and top with the Parmesan.

An oakleaf lettuce salad makes a crisp, sharp
contrast to the succulent risotto. If you cannot
find dried ceps, or porcini as they are called in
Italian delicatessen, use an extra 2oz (60g)
of button mushrooms.

ONE SERVING

CALORIES 450

TOTAL FAT 16g

SATURATED FAT 5g

CARBOHYDRATES 59g

ADDED SUGAR 0

FIBRE 2g

SODIUM 175mg

Wild rice and mushrooms give extra taste and texture to a delicious risotto, whose flavour is dominated by the light and crumbly chicken livers.

Paella

SERVES 6
PREPARATION TIME: 35 minutes
COOKING TIME: 1 hour

ONE SERVING

CALORIES 425

TOTAL FAT 10g

SATURATED FAT 2g

CARBOHYDRATES 52g

ADDED SUGAR 0

FIBRE 3g

SODIUM 460mg

TIP
To ensure that the whole dish is enhanced by the subtle saffron, steep the strands in a cupful of heated stock for 10 minutes. Add to the dish with the rest of the stock.

1 pint (570ml) fresh mussels
2 tablespoons olive oil
2 boneless chicken breasts, each about 8oz (225g), skinned and cut into 3 equal pieces
1 medium onion, peeled and finely chopped
1 medium fennel bulb, trimmed and finely chopped
1 clove garlic, peeled and finely chopped
1 small red pepper, de-seeded and chopped
12oz (340g) Valencia or long-grain white rice
½ level teaspoon saffron strands
1¼ pints (725ml) chicken stock
1 bay leaf
8oz (225g) cleaned fresh squid, cut into rings
4oz (115g) unpeeled prawns
2oz (60g) peeled prawns
4oz (115g) frozen petits pois
Freshly ground black pepper
Chopped fennel fronds to garnish

1   Scrub the mussels well, remove the beards and put the mussels in cold water until needed.

2   Heat the oil in a paella pan or large, flameproof casserole. Fry the chicken pieces in it for 15 minutes, turning frequently. Drain the chicken on kitchen paper and keep hot.

3   Put the onion, fennel, garlic and red pepper in the pan and cook over a moderate heat for 5 minutes, until softening. Mix in the rice and cook over a low heat for 5 minutes, stirring. Add the saffron and stock, and stir until it boils. Put in the chicken pieces and bay leaf, and simmer, uncovered, for 15 minutes.

4   Mix in the squid and drained mussels, cover and simmer for about 8 minutes, until the squid is tender and the mussels are open. Discard any mussels that remain closed.

5   Stir in the prawns and peas and cook gently for 5 minutes more, stirring occasionally. Remove the bay leaf, season with pepper and garnish with fennel fronds.

Serve a light, leafy salad as a foil for the varied flavours of the paella.

The ingredients in this Spanish dish vary with the seasons, but the hearty blend always includes a variety of seafoods in plump golden rice.

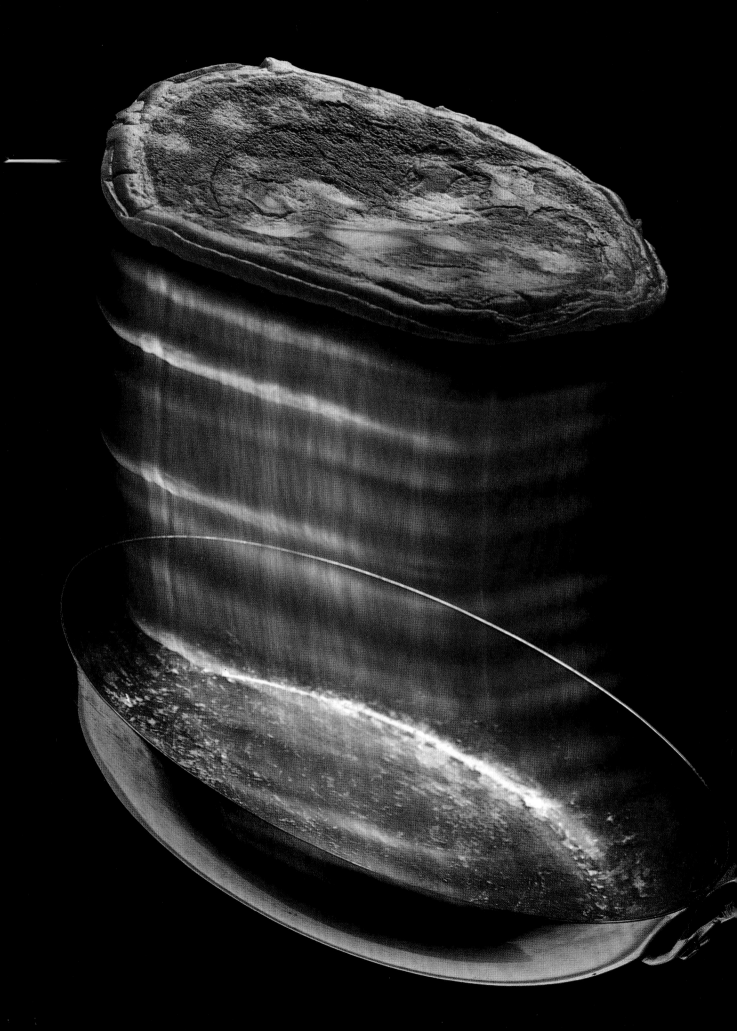

VEGETARIAN DISHES

Growing numbers of people are narrowing down the types of protein they eat, but these recipes show that the range of dishes without meat or fish is far from narrow. By combining peas, beans or lentils with nuts or grain and varying them with dairy foods, you will get plenty of protein. Add a dash of adventure and the range of mouthwatering possibilities widens – pies and hotpots, paella and pancakes, curries and quiches – and there is a whole new repertoire of meals not just for vegetarian visitors but for the family as well.

Aubergine and cheese gratin

SERVES 4
PREPARATION TIME: 25 minutes
COOKING TIME: 45 minutes
OVEN: Preheat to 180°C (350°F, gas mark 4)

1 tablespoon olive oil
2 tablespoons lemon juice
1lb (450g) aubergines, trimmed and thickly sliced
14oz (400g) tinned tomatoes, sieved
14oz (400g) tinned chopped tomatoes
2 cloves garlic, peeled and crushed

1 level teaspoon dried oregano
1 level tablespoon chopped fresh basil
2oz (60g) grated Parmesan cheese
1oz (30g) wholemeal breadcrumbs
4oz (115g) ricotta cheese
1oz (30g) mozzarella cheese, grated or thinly sliced

1 Mix the oil and lemon juice together and brush both sides of the aubergine slices with the mixture. Grill them for 2 minutes on each side under a high heat until golden brown.

2 Bring the sieved tomatoes and chopped tomatoes to the boil in a saucepan and stir in the garlic and oregano. Boil briskly for about 5 minutes until reduced by a third. Remove from the heat and stir in the basil.

3 Mix the Parmesan with the breadcrumbs in a small bowl. Spread a third of the tomato mixture over the bottom of an ovenproof dish and sprinkle on half the breadcrumb mixture. Arrange half the aubergine slices over the top and crumble half the ricotta over them. Repeat these layers and spread the remaining tomato mixture on top. Cover with the mozzarella.

4 Cook in the heated oven for 45 minutes, or until bubbling hot and browned on top.

Serve the gratin piping hot with granary bread.

Grilling the aubergine slices before they go in the gratin gives them extra flavour to add to the layers of basil and tomato sauce and three Italian cheeses.

ONE SERVING
CALORIES 210
TOTAL FAT 14g
SATURATED FAT 4g
CARBOHYDRATES 10g
ADDED SUGAR 0
FIBRE 3g
SODIUM 305mg

Stuffed aubergines

ONE SERVING
CALORIES 280
TOTAL FAT 18g
SATURATED FAT 4g
CARBOHYDRATES 21g
ADDED SUGAR 0
FIBRE 6g
SODIUM 270mg

SERVES 4
PREPARATION TIME: 30 minutes
COOKING TIME: 20 minutes
OVEN: Preheat to 200°C (400°F, gas mark 6)

2 aubergines, each about 8oz (225g), trimmed
1 tablespoon olive oil
1 medium onion, peeled and finely chopped
2 cloves garlic, peeled and crushed
4oz (115g) mushrooms, wiped and finely chopped
1 large carrot, peeled and coarsely grated

2 level teaspoons dried basil
1 level teaspoon dried marjoram
4oz (115g) fresh wholemeal breadcrumbs
1oz (30g) macadamia or brazil nuts, roughly chopped
1 level tablespoon sunflower seeds
1 level tablespoon pumpkin seeds
Freshly ground black pepper
3oz (85g) soft goat's cheese, thinly sliced
1 level tablespoon pine nuts
Sprigs of fresh marjoram to garnish

1 Halve the aubergines lengthways and scoop out the flesh with a teaspoon, leaving the shells about ¼ in (6mm) thick. Blanch the shells in boiling water for 2 minutes, then drain.

2 Heat the oil in a saucepan and cook the onion and garlic in it over a moderate heat for 5 minutes until lightly browned. Stir in the mushrooms, carrot, basil and marjoram. Chop the aubergine flesh and mix it in with the vegetables. Cook gently for about 10 minutes, uncovered, stirring frequently. Mix in the breadcrumbs, chopped nuts and sunflower and pumpkin seeds, and season with pepper.

3 Arrange the aubergine shells in a lightly oiled baking dish and fill with the stuffing. Top each with cheese slices and sprinkle with pine nuts. Bake in the heated oven for 20 minutes, or until the cheese has melted and the stuffing is hot all through. Garnish with the marjoram sprigs before serving.

Large, boat-shaped aubergine shells are delicious containers for a savoury vegetable, nut and herb stuffing. Pine nuts and sunflower and pumpkin seeds add a crunchy element to this moist Mediterranean-style dish, and the goat's-cheese topping gives a tart finish.

Bean and aubergine moussaka

ONE SERVING	
CALORIES	370
TOTAL FAT	16g
SATURATED FAT	4g
CARBOHYDRATES	36g
ADDED SUGAR	0
FIBRE	9g
SODIUM	240mg

SERVES 4
PREPARATION TIME: 30 minutes
COOKING TIME: 40 minutes
OVEN: Preheat to 180°C (350°F, gas mark 4)

3oz (85g) split red lentils, cleaned of grit, rinsed and drained
2 tablespoons olive oil
1 tablespoon lemon juice
1lb (450g) aubergines, trimmed and thickly sliced
1 medium onion, peeled and chopped

1 clove garlic, peeled and crushed
2oz (60g) mushrooms, wiped and finely chopped
1 level teaspoon dried thyme
¼ level teaspoon ground cinnamon
14oz (400g) tinned chopped tomatoes
2 tablespoons tomato purée
Freshly ground black pepper
8oz (225g) cooked red kidney beans
3 eggs, size 2, beaten
10oz (275g) low-fat natural yoghurt
½ oz (15g) grated Parmesan cheese

Kidney beans, lentils and mushrooms replace the lamb of a Greek moussaka, but the melting aubergines are kept.

TIP
For a fluffy topping, separate one of the eggs, whisk the white and fold it into the egg and yoghurt mixture just before pouring it onto the aubergines.

1 Simmer the lentils for 20 minutes in unsalted water. Meanwhile, mix half the oil with the lemon juice. Lay the aubergines on a grill rack and brush both sides with the oil and lemon. Cook under a medium grill for about 2 minutes each side, until golden, and set aside.

2 Heat the remaining oil in a saucepan and cook the onion and garlic in it over a moderate heat for 5 minutes, until softened. Stir in the

mushrooms, thyme, cinnamon, tomatoes and tomato purée and simmer for 5 minutes.

3 When the lentils are tender, drain them, season with pepper and mix into the tomatoes.

4 Lay half the aubergine slices in an ovenproof dish. Spread half the beans on top and cover with the tomato mixture. Top with the rest of the beans, then the rest of the aubergine slices.

5 Mix the eggs into the yoghurt and season with pepper. Pour the mixture over the aubergine slices. Sprinkle with the Parmesan and bake in the heated oven for about 40 minutes, until bubbling and browned.

A salad of finely sliced onion and white cabbage, tossed in a lemon vinaigrette dressing, provides a sharp, crisp contrast to the soft, moist moussaka. Serve warm crusty bread for mopping up the sauce.

Broccoli and Cheddar soufflé

ONE SERVING
....
CALORIES 225
....
TOTAL FAT 15g
....
SATURATED FAT 8g
....
CARBOHYDRATES 10g
....
ADDED SUGAR 0
....
FIBRE 2g
....
SODIUM 255mg
....

TIP
Be sure to steam the broccoli only lightly so that it does not become soggy. Waterlogged broccoli will spoil the soufflé's rise.

Firm morsels of steamed broccoli make a well-flavoured addition in this fluffy soufflé. Their slightly peppery taste is intensified by mustard and cayenne pepper.

SERVES 4
PREPARATION TIME: 30 minutes
COOKING TIME: 35 minutes
OVEN: Preheat to 200°C (400°F, gas mark 6)

½oz (15g) slightly salted butter
3 level tablespoons plain flour
8fl oz (225ml) skimmed milk
1 bay leaf
2 whole eggs, separated, plus 3 egg whites, size 2
1 level teaspoon made English mustard
3oz (85g) finely grated mature Cheddar cheese
7oz (200g) broccoli, very lightly steamed and finely chopped
¼ level teaspoon cayenne pepper

1 Melt the butter in a saucepan, stir in the flour, cook gently for 1 minute and take off the heat. Gradually stir in the milk, put in the bay leaf and then bring to the boil over a moderate heat, stirring continuously. Simmer for about 2 minutes, until the sauce thickens.

2 Remove from the heat, discard the bay leaf and beat in the egg yolks. Stir in the mustard, Cheddar, broccoli and cayenne pepper.

3 Lightly grease a deep soufflé dish 7in (18cm) in diameter. Whisk the egg whites until they stay in soft peaks when you pull up the whisk. Using a metal spoon, fold 2 tablespoons of the egg whites into the cheese sauce, then fold in the rest. Spoon into the soufflé dish and cook in the heated oven for about 35 minutes, or until risen and golden brown. Serve at once.

Butter-bean hotpot

ONE SERVING	
CALORIES	290
TOTAL FAT	8g
SATURATED FAT	2g
CARBOHYDRATES	42g
ADDED SUGAR	0
FIBRE	16g
SODIUM	115mg

SERVES 4
PREPARATION TIME: 15 minutes
COOKING TIME: 1 hour 40 minutes

4oz (115g) butter beans, soaked in cold water overnight (see p.17)
1¼ pints (725ml) vegetable stock
8 button onions, peeled, or 2 medium onions, peeled and thickly sliced
8oz (225g) swede, peeled and cut into cubes
8oz (225g) parsnips, peeled, quartered lengthways and thickly sliced
8oz (225g) carrots, peeled and cut into chunks
2 sprigs thyme
2 bay leaves
4 level tablespoons chopped fresh parsley
2 sprigs tarragon
3oz (85g) shelled broad beans, or frozen broad beans, rinsed
1 tablespoon corn oil
1 level tablespoon plain wholemeal flour
4oz (115g) medium-fat soft cheese
Freshly ground black pepper
Parsley sprigs to garnish

1 Rinse and drain the butter beans and put them into a large saucepan with the stock. Bring to the boil and skim off any scum that rises. Put on the lid and simmer for about 1 hour, until the beans begin to soften.

2 Stir in the onions, swede, parsnips, carrots, thyme, bay leaves, parsley and tarragon, and simmer, covered, for 20 minutes. Mix in the broad beans and cook for a further 10 minutes, until all the vegetables are tender. Remove from the heat and pour off the stock into a measuring jug. Remove the thyme, bay leaves and tarragon from the pan. Leave the pan off the heat with the lid on.

3 Keep ½ pint (285ml) of the stock, topping up with water if necessary. Heat the oil in a small saucepan, mix in the flour, then gradually stir in the stock. Bring to the boil, stirring, then reduce the heat and simmer for 2-3 minutes. Remove from the heat, whisk in the cheese and season with the pepper. Pour the sauce over the vegetables and reheat gently, stirring carefully, then turn into a warm serving dish and garnish with the parsley sprigs.

Serve the hotpot with crusty wholemeal bread. You can vary the fresh herbs according to what is available. Shallots or leeks and celeriac can replace the onions and parsnips, and you can add mushrooms to vary the dish.

This comforting winter hotpot brims with vegetables, including fibre-rich broad beans and butter beans, and will satisfy the healthiest of appetites.

Cabbage noodle casserole

SERVES 4
PREPARATION TIME: 10 minutes
COOKING TIME: 25 minutes

1 tablespoon olive oil
1 medium onion, peeled and chopped
1lb (450g) savoy cabbage, trimmed and shredded
½ level teaspoon caraway seeds
½ level teaspoon celery seeds
4fl oz (115ml) dry white wine
Freshly ground black pepper
4oz (115g) Chinese egg noodles
2 level tablespoons cornflour
¾ pint (425ml) vegetable stock
4oz (115g) Greek yoghurt
2oz (60g) flaked almonds
1oz (30g) wholemeal breadcrumbs
1oz (30g) grated Parmesan cheese
Marjoram sprigs to garnish

ONE SERVING	
CALORIES	380
TOTAL FAT	20g
SATURATED FAT	4g
CARBOHYDRATES	36g
ADDED SUGAR	0
FIBRE	6g
SODIUM	200mg

Crinkly, crisp shreds of savoy cabbage give a lively flavour, colour and texture to this casserole, which is moistened by a smooth yoghurt sauce flavoured with white wine and caraway and celery seeds.

1 Heat the oil in a heavy-based saucepan and cook the onion in it over a moderate heat for 5 minutes to brown. Stir in the cabbage, caraway and celery seeds, and wine, and season with pepper. Cover and simmer for 10 minutes.

2 Cook the noodles in unsalted water.

3 Blend the cornflour with 2 tablespoons of stock. Mix with the rest of the stock, pour onto the cabbage and stir over a low heat until it thickens. Mix in the yoghurt and noodles, turn into a wide heatproof dish and top with almonds, breadcrumbs and Parmesan. Brown under a moderate grill and garnish with the marjoram.

Carrot and rice terrine

SERVES 6
PREPARATION TIME: 35 minutes
COOKING TIME: 50 minutes
OVEN: Preheat to 180°C (350°F, gas mark 4)

ONE SERVING

CALORIES 360

TOTAL FAT 20g

SATURATED FAT 6g

CARBOHYDRATES 35g

ADDED SUGAR 0

FIBRE 2g

SODIUM 175mg

Plump, firm brown rice, chewy, aromatic wild rice and tender, sweet carrots combine in a terrine enriched with walnuts and the savour of mature cheese.

1 pint (570ml) vegetable stock
4oz (115g) brown rice
4oz (115g) wild rice mixture
2 tablespoons olive oil
1 large onion, peeled and finely chopped
2 sticks celery, trimmed and finely chopped
4 medium carrots, peeled and grated
3 level tablespoons chopped fresh parsley
2 eggs, size 2, lightly beaten
2oz (60g) chopped walnuts
2 level teaspoons ground cumin
4oz (115g) grated mature Cheddar cheese
Freshly ground black pepper

1 Bring the stock to the boil in a large saucepan, stir in all the rice and simmer, covered, for about 15 minutes, until the rice has absorbed most of the liquid. Turn the heat very low and continue cooking, covered, for 5 minutes, stirring occasionally.

2 Meanwhile, heat the oil in a frying pan and cook the onion and celery in it over a moderate heat for about 5 minutes. Mix in the carrots and cook for 3 minutes. Leave to cool slightly.

3 Stir the vegetables into the rice and mix in the parsley, eggs, walnuts, cumin and 3oz (85g) of the Cheddar. Season with pepper.

4 Turn the mixture into a lightly oiled loaf tin about 10×5in (25×13cm) and sprinkle with the remaining Cheddar. Cook in the heated oven for about 50 minutes, until golden and firm to the touch. Let the terrine cool for 10 minutes before turning it out of the tin.

Slice the terrine to serve hot with a green vegetable or cold with a leafy salad.

The concentrated flavours of Gruyère and spring onions make a piquant contrast to the gentle taste of fresh ricotta in this warming pie.

Cheese and potato pie

ONE SERVING

CALORIES 350

TOTAL FAT 18g

SATURATED FAT 10g

CARBOHYDRATES 32g

ADDED SUGAR 0

FIBRE 3g

SODIUM 290mg

SERVES 4
PREPARATION TIME: 15 minutes
COOKING TIME: 30 minutes
OVEN: Preheat to 200°C (400°F, gas mark 6)

1½ lb (680g) potatoes, peeled
6oz (175g) ricotta cheese
1 egg, size 2
Freshly ground black pepper
1 teaspoon olive oil
4 spring onions, trimmed and chopped
2oz (60g) finely grated Gruyère cheese

1 Boil the potatoes in unsalted water until cooked but still firm. Drain and slice thinly.

2 Blend the ricotta with the egg and season with pepper.

3 Brush an ovenproof dish with the oil. Layer a third of the sliced potatoes over the bottom of the dish, spread on half the ricotta mixture and sprinkle a third of the spring onion and Gruyère on top. Repeat the layers, then cover with the rest of the potato and sprinkle the remaining spring onions and Gruyère on top. Cook in the heated oven for about 30 minutes, until golden brown on top.

Cheese and vegetable pudding

ONE SERVING
....
CALORIES 365
....
TOTAL FAT 15g
....
SATURATED FAT 5g
....
CARBOHYDRATES 40g
....
ADDED SUGAR 0
....
FIBRE 5g
....
SODIUM 630mg
....

SERVES 4
PREPARATION TIME: 15 minutes, plus 1 hour to stand
COOKING TIME: 40 minutes
OVEN: Preheat to 160°C (325°F, gas mark 3)

1 tablespoon olive oil
1 small onion, peeled and chopped
1 small stick celery, trimmed and chopped
½ small green or red pepper, de-seeded and finely chopped

2 tomatoes, skinned, de-seeded and chopped
3oz (85g) frozen sweetcorn kernels, rinsed
8 slices wholemeal bread, about ¼ in (6mm) thick, cut into quarters
1oz (30g) grated Gruyère cheese
2 eggs, plus 1 egg white, size 2
12fl oz (340ml) skimmed milk
¾ level teaspoon mustard powder
¾ level teaspoon paprika
⅛ level teaspoon cayenne pepper
1oz (30g) grated Parmesan cheese

Layers of wholemeal bread triangles and a brilliantly coloured medley of crunchy chopped vegetables give body to this savoury cheese custard.

1 Heat the oil in a frying pan and cook the onion, celery and green or red pepper in it over a moderate heat for 5 minutes until they are beginning to soften. Take off the heat and stir in the tomatoes and sweetcorn.

2 Lightly grease a shallow ovenproof dish and arrange the bread in it in overlapping layers. Spoon the vegetable mixture evenly over the bread and sprinkle the Gruyère on top.

3 Whisk the eggs and egg white with the milk, mustard, paprika and cayenne. Slowly pour into the dish without moving the bread. Put in the refrigerator for 1 hour for the bread to soak.

4 Sprinkle the Parmesan on the top and cook in the heated oven for 40 minutes, or until set.

A salad of lamb's lettuce, beetroot and celery makes a contrast with the dish.

Chilli with rice

SERVES 4
PREPARATION TIME: 10 minutes
COOKING TIME: 1 hour 10 minutes

1½ tablespoons olive oil
1 large onion, peeled and chopped
1 large carrot, peeled and chopped
3 cloves garlic, peeled and finely chopped
1 green pepper, de-seeded and chopped
1 red pepper, de-seeded and chopped
4oz (115g) green lentils, cleaned of grit, washed
and drained
½ level teaspoon chilli powder
1 level teaspoon ground cumin
1 bay leaf
⅛ level teaspoon cayenne pepper
14oz (400g) tinned chopped tomatoes
¾ pint (425ml) vegetable stock
6oz (175g) long-grain rice
8oz (225g) cooked red kidney beans
8oz (225g) cooked chickpeas
Coriander or parsley sprigs to garnish

ONE SERVING

CALORIES 565

TOTAL FAT 11g

SATURATED FAT 1g

CARBOHYDRATES 94g

ADDED SUGAR 0

FIBRE 16g

SODIUM 60mg

1 Heat the oil in a heavy-based saucepan and cook the onion, carrot, garlic and green and red peppers in it over a moderate heat for 10 minutes, until the vegetables are softened.

2 Add the lentils, chilli powder, cumin, bay leaf, cayenne pepper, tomatoes and stock. Cover and simmer for 50 minutes.

3 Meanwhile, cook the rice.

4 Stir the kidney beans and chickpeas into the lentil mixture, cover and simmer for a further 10 minutes, until the lentils are tender but not mushy. Remove the bay leaf.

5 Spoon the rice into individual serving bowls with a helping of the chilli on top. Garnish with the coriander or parsley.

A salad of cucumber with yoghurt and mint makes a cooling side dish for the spicy chilli.

This substantial dish combines sweet peppers and tomatoes with fiery chilli and cayenne pepper to make a sauce for fibre-rich lentils, beans and chickpeas.

Cottage cheese and basil quiche

ONE SERVING

CALORIES 325

TOTAL FAT 18g

SATURATED FAT 5g

CARBOHYDRATES 25g

ADDED SUGAR 0

FIBRE 3g

SODIUM 380mg

TIP
If the top of the quiche is browning too quickly, lay a piece of greaseproof paper loosely on top. Do not lower the temperature or the pastry under the quiche will not be cooked crisp.

SERVES 4
PREPARATION TIME: 25 minutes
COOKING TIME: 25 minutes
OVEN: Preheat to 200°C (400°F, gas mark 6)

1 medium courgette, trimmed and thinly sliced
3 tablespoons water
2oz (60g) plain white flour
2oz (60g) wholemeal flour
2oz (60g) polyunsaturated margarine
2 eggs, size 2, separated
8oz (225g) cottage cheese, well drained
3 level tablespoons chopped fresh basil
4 spring onions, trimmed and chopped
2oz (60g) frozen sweetcorn kernels, rinsed
Freshly ground black pepper
Basil leaves to garnish

1 Simmer the courgette with 2 tablespoons of the water in a small, covered saucepan for 5 minutes until softening. Drain and set aside.

2 Mix the flours in a bowl and rub in the margarine with your fingertips until the mixture resembles fine breadcrumbs. Use a round-ended knife to work in 1 egg yolk and just enough of the remaining water to form a dough.

3 Knead the dough on a lightly floured surface, then roll it out to fit a fluted flan tin 8½ in (21.5cm) in diameter. Line the tin with the pastry, smoothing it out from the centre and pressing it well into the flutes to make sure no air is trapped underneath. Trim the excess pastry from the edge.

4 Mix the cottage cheese, basil, courgette, onions, sweetcorn and the remaining egg yolk, and season with pepper. Whisk the egg whites until they hold soft peaks, then carefully fold them into the cheese mixture.

5 Place the pastry-lined flan tin on a baking sheet and pour in the filling. Cook in the heated oven for about 25 minutes, or until the pastry is golden brown and the filling set. Garnish with basil before serving hot or cold.

A crisp green salad goes well with the delicately flavoured quiche.

Cottage cheese gives a beautifully light texture to this quiche, while pungent fresh basil creates an irresistible aroma. You can prepare the pastry case one day in advance and put it, uncooked, in a polythene bag in the refrigerator until needed.

Courgette and carrot quiche

ONE SERVING

CALORIES 260

TOTAL FAT 9g

SATURATED FAT 5g

CARBOHYDRATES 32g

ADDED SUGAR 0

FIBRE 1g

SODIUM 242mg

SERVES 4
PREPARATION TIME: 45 minutes
COOKING TIME: 20 minutes, plus 15 minutes to rest
OVEN: Preheat to 180° (350°F, gas mark 4)

1 medium onion, peeled and finely chopped
1 medium carrot, peeled and grated
1 medium courgette, trimmed and grated
½ level teaspoon dried marjoram
7fl oz (200ml) vegetable stock
6oz (175g) arborio or long-grain rice
3oz (85g) grated Gruyère cheese
3 egg whites, plus 1 whole egg, size 2
2 level teaspoons cornflour
¼ pint (150ml) skimmed milk
Freshly ground black pepper
Marjoram sprigs to garnish

1   Simmer the onion, carrot, courgette and marjoram in the stock, uncovered, for 15 minutes. Raise the heat and boil briskly for about 10 minutes, stirring frequently, until the liquid has evaporated and the vegetables are almost glazed.

2   Meanwhile, cook the rice, and line a straight-sided, spring-clip tin 8½ in (21.5cm) in diameter with nonstick baking paper.

3   Mix the rice thoroughly with 2 tablespoons of the Gruyère and 1 egg white. Spread the mixture over the base and up the sides of the flan tin, pressing it well with the back of a spoon. Bake in the heated oven for 5 minutes, then lift out and leave to cool slightly, still in the tin.

4   Mix the cornflour to a smooth, thin cream with a little of the milk, then stir in the remaining milk and whisk in the whole egg and remaining egg whites. Add the remaining Gruyère, season with pepper and cook over a very low heat, stirring continuously, until the custard thickens.

5   Spread the vegetables in the flan case, pour on the custard and cook in the heated oven for 20 minutes, until the filling is set. Leave to rest for 15 minutes before removing very carefully from the tin and garnishing with marjoram.

Sliced tomatoes and cucumber sprinkled with lemon juice and mixed fresh herbs add sharpness and colour to the quiche.

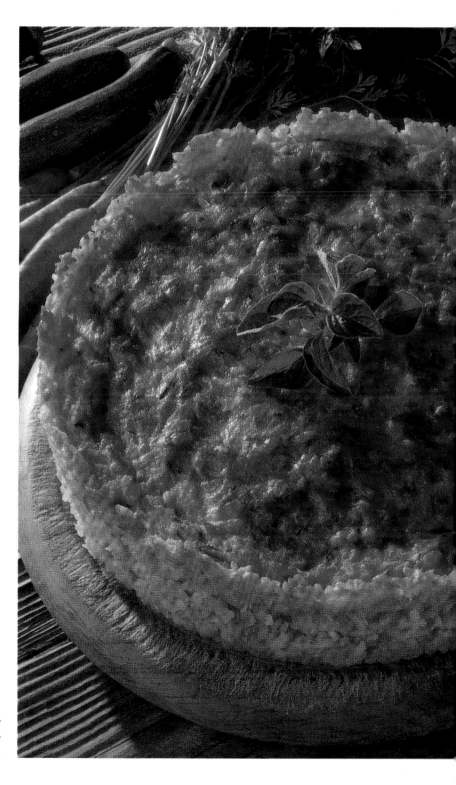

The extra care needed to make the case and filling are amply rewarded by this quiche with its delicately flavoured filling set in a crisp, light crust of rice.

Curried vegetables with cucumber sauce

ONE SERVING

CALORIES 325

TOTAL FAT 6g

SATURATED FAT 1g

CARBOHYDRATES 59g

ADDED SUGAR 0

FIBRE 7g

SODIUM 85mg

SERVES 4
PREPARATION TIME: 15 minutes
COOKING TIME: 40 minutes

4oz (115g) cauliflower florets
1 tablespoon olive oil
1 onion, peeled and chopped
2 cloves garlic, peeled and crushed

1 level tablespoon medium or hot curry powder
½ level teaspoon ground cinnamon
1 pint (570ml) vegetable stock
4oz (115g) long-grain rice
2 medium tomatoes, skinned and chopped
2 carrots, peeled and chopped
8oz (225g) cooked black-eyed or butter beans
(see p.17)
2oz (60g) raisins
4oz (115g) frozen peas
2 teaspoons lemon juice
2 level tablespoons chopped fresh coriander leaves

For the sauce:
8oz (225g) low-fat natural yoghurt
2oz (60g) grated cucumber
Freshly ground black pepper
¼ level teaspoon paprika
Fresh mint to garnish

1 Blanch the cauliflower in boiling water for 2 minutes, then drain and set aside.

2 Heat the oil in a large, heavy-based saucepan and cook the onion in it for 5 minutes over a moderate heat, until golden. Stir in the garlic, curry powder and cinnamon and cook for 30 seconds, stirring.

3 Add the stock, rice, tomatoes and carrots to the pan and bring to the boil. Cover and simmer for 20 minutes. Stir in the beans, raisins, peas and cauliflower, cover and cook for 8 minutes more.

4 Meanwhile, mix the yoghurt and cucumber and season with pepper to make the sauce. Turn it into a small serving bowl, dust with the paprika and garnish with mint.

5 Stir the lemon juice and coriander into the curry and spoon it into a heated serving dish.

Individual side dishes of skinned tomato wedges and grated celeriac sprinkled with lemon juice make cooling accompaniments to offer with the curry.

Yoghurt is often served plain as a foil to searing curries in the Middle East and Asia. It is especially refreshing when, as in this dish, it is combined with cucumber to make an Indian-style 'raita'.

A speciality of Middle Eastern cookery, spicy chickpea patties served with crisp salad in pockets of pitta bread are filling and easy to make.

Falafel in pitta bread

ONE SERVING	
CALORIES 460	
TOTAL FAT 12g	
SATURATED FAT 1g	
CARBOHYDRATES 75g	
ADDED SUGAR 0	
FIBRE 9g	
SODIUM 540mg	

TIP
Wash and dry the lettuce 30 minutes before it is needed and refrigerate it in an airtight plastic box to make it especially crisp.

SERVES 4
PREPARATION TIME: 25 minutes
COOKING TIME: 10 minutes

10oz (275g) cooked chickpeas
1 level teaspoon ground cumin
1 level teaspoon ground coriander
2 cloves garlic, peeled and chopped
¼ level teaspoon cayenne pepper
2 teaspoons groundnut oil
3 tablespoons lemon juice
⅛ level teaspoon salt
6oz (175g) low-fat natural yoghurt
1 tablespoon olive oil
8-10 leaves of cos-type lettuce, washed and torn into pieces
8oz (225g) ripe tomatoes, skinned, de-seeded and diced
4 wholemeal oval pitta breads
1 level tablespoon sesame seeds, lightly toasted

1 Using a food processor or food mill, blend the chickpeas, cumin, coriander, garlic, cayenne pepper, groundnut oil, 2 tablespoons of the lemon juice and the salt to a smooth

purée. If the mixture is too dry to hold together, mix in 2-3 teaspoons cold water.

2 Divide the mixture into eight and shape the pieces into flat, round patties, or falafel. Lightly grease a nonstick frying pan with groundnut oil and cook the falafel in it over a moderate heat for 4 minutes on each side, until golden brown and crisp.

3 Meanwhile, whisk together the yoghurt and olive oil with the remaining lemon juice. Set aside 4 tablespoons of this dressing. Pour the rest over the lettuce and tomatoes, and toss to coat well.

4 Slit each pitta bread open along one side only, and fill with 2 falafel and a quarter of the salad mixture. Trickle 1 tablespoon of the reserved dressing into each pitta, sprinkle with the sesame seeds and serve at once.

Diced pickled beetroot, perhaps mixed with cucumber, makes a sharp and refreshing side dish for the falafel.

Fennel and potato hotpot

ONE SERVING	
CALORIES	235
TOTAL FAT	8g
SATURATED FAT	3g
CARBOHYDRATES	22g
ADDED SUGAR	0
FIBRE	4g
SODIUM	195mg

SERVES 4
PREPARATION TIME: 20 minutes
COOKING TIME: 40 minutes
OVEN: Preheat to 200°C (400°F, gas mark 6)

1lb (450g) fennel bulbs, trimmed and thickly sliced
2 cloves garlic, peeled and finely chopped
2 level tablespoons chopped fresh parsley

1 level teaspoon crushed fennel seeds
1lb (450g) potatoes, peeled and thinly sliced
1 tablespoon olive oil
3oz (85g) grated reduced-fat Cheddar cheese
Freshly ground black pepper
7fl oz (200ml) dry white wine
2 level tablespoons grated Parmesan cheese
Fennel fronds to garnish

1 Cook the fennel in boiling, unsalted water for 10 minutes, then drain thoroughly and mix in the garlic, parsley, fennel seeds and potatoes.

2 Grease an ovenproof dish with half the olive oil and spread half the vegetables in the dish. Sprinkle on the Cheddar and spread the rest of the vegetables over the top. Season with pepper, pour in the wine and remaining olive oil and scatter the Parmesan over the top.

3 Bake in the heated oven for 40 minutes, or until the top is crisp and golden brown and the vegetables are tender. Garnish with the fennel fronds just before serving.

A tomato and cucumber salad dressed with lemon juice makes a sharp contrast to the mild aniseed flavour of the fennel.

Fennel bulbs are often eaten crisp and raw in salads, but they are particularly satisfying when cooked until tender and lending their flavour to other vegetables.

Gougère ring filled with ratatouille

ONE SERVING	
CALORIES	360
TOTAL FAT	26g
SATURATED FAT	8g
CARBOHYDRATES	21g
ADDED SUGAR	0
FIBRE	4g
SODIUM	290mg

SERVES 4
PREPARATION TIME: 30 minutes
COOKING TIME: 40 minutes
OVEN: Preheat to 220°C (425°F gas mark 7)

For the gougère:
¼ pint (150ml) water
2oz (60g) polyunsaturated margarine
2½ oz (70g) mixed plain white and wholemeal flour, or all wholemeal flour
2 eggs, size 3, beaten
2oz (60g) finely grated Gruyère cheese

For the ratatouille:
1 tablespoon olive oil
1 medium onion, peeled and sliced
1 medium aubergine, trimmed and chopped
2 courgettes, trimmed and sliced
½ green pepper, de-seeded and chopped
½ red pepper, de-seeded and chopped
1lb (450g) firm red tomatoes, chopped
1 tablespoon tomato purée
1 level teaspoon dried basil
Freshly ground black pepper
Basil or oregano sprigs to garnish

1 Put the water and margarine into a saucepan and bring to the boil slowly, so that the margarine melts before the water boils. Take the pan off the heat and quickly tip in all the flour. Beat well with a wooden spoon until the paste forms a ball that rolls cleanly round the pan. Leave for 5 minutes.

2 Gradually beat the eggs into the cooled paste, using a hand-held electric mixer or a wooden spoon, then beat in three-quarters of the Gruyère. Place spoonfuls of the mixture touching one another in a ring inside the rim of an ovenproof dish 9in (23cm) in diameter. Sprinkle with the remaining Gruyère. Bake in the heated oven for 20 minutes, then reduce the heat to 190°C (375°F, gas mark 5) and cook for a further 10 minutes.

3 Meanwhile, prepare the ratatouille. Heat the oil in a large saucepan and cook the onion in it over a moderate heat for 5 minutes. Mix in the aubergine, courgettes, green and red peppers, tomatoes, tomato purée and dried basil, and season with pepper. Cover and cook, stirring occasionally, for 20 minutes or until tender.

4 Fill the centre of the ring with ratatouille and garnish with basil or oregano sprigs.

A simple leafy salad is all that is needed with the puffy ring and moist filling.

Airy choux pastry flavoured with cheese is used for gougères. Here this French delicacy from Burgundy is made into a ring to hold a colourful ratatouille.

Lentil, split pea and nut rissoles

ONE SERVING	
CALORIES 285	
TOTAL FAT 14g	
SATURATED FAT 2g	
CARBOHYDRATES 30g	
ADDED SUGAR 0	
FIBRE 4g	
SODIUM 35mg	

SERVES 4
PREPARATION TIME: 20 minutes, plus 8 hours to soak
COOKING TIME: 25 minutes

2oz (60g) split red lentils, cleaned, soaked in cold water for 8 hours and drained
4oz (115g) yellow split peas, soaked in cold water for 8 hours and drained

2oz (60g) skinned hazelnuts, toasted
¼ level teaspoon ground coriander
2 level tablespoons chopped fresh coriander
Finely grated rind of 1 small lemon
1 clove garlic, peeled and crushed
¼ level teaspoon bicarbonate of soda
2 level tablespoons plain wholemeal flour
2 tablespoons groundnut oil
Lemon wedges and coriander sprigs to garnish

Coriander, garlic and toasted hazelnuts give a tempting aroma to this version of a vegetarian favourite. Crisp and brown outside, chewy within, these rissoles make a satisfying dish.

1 Grind the lentils and peas in a food processor for about 25 seconds, until finely ground. Add the hazelnuts and blend again for about 10 seconds.

2 Turn the mixture into a bowl and work in the ground and chopped coriander, lemon rind, garlic, bicarbonate of soda and flour.

3 Divide the mixture into 12 equal portions. Roll each portion between wetted palms into a ball, then flatten slightly.

4 Heat the oil in a large, nonstick frying pan and fry the rissoles in it over a moderate heat for 5 minutes, turning two or three times, until well browned. Drain on kitchen paper. If the frying pan will not hold the rissoles easily, cook them in two batches and keep the first batch hot while you fry the second.

Serve the rissoles garnished with the lemon wedges and coriander leaves. A salad of chicory, watercress and rocket leaves will add a peppery touch to the mild flavours of the rissoles.

Lentil and potato stew

SERVES 6
PREPARATION TIME: 30 minutes
COOKING TIME: 1 hour

1½ pints (850ml) vegetable stock
8oz (225g) red lentils, cleaned of grit and rinsed
1 medium onion, peeled and chopped
2 cloves garlic, peeled and finely chopped
2 sticks celery, trimmed and sliced
4 carrots, peeled and cut into fingers
1¾ lb (800g) tinned chopped tomatoes
1 level teaspoon chopped fresh rosemary,
or ½ level teaspoon dried rosemary
1 tablespoon olive oil
16 button onions, peeled
1lb (450g) potatoes, peeled and cut into cubes
Freshly ground black pepper
4oz (115g) button mushrooms, wiped and halved
1 level tablespoon chopped fresh parsley

1 Put the stock, lentils, chopped onion, garlic, celery, carrots, tomatoes and rosemary into a large saucepan, bring to the boil and skim off any scum. Cover and simmer for 35 minutes.

2 Meanwhile, heat the oil in a frying pan and brown the button onions in it over a moderate heat for 5 minutes, shaking the pan frequently.

3 Mix the button onions and the potatoes into the lentils and vegetables, cover and simmer for a further 15-20 minutes, until the lentils and potatoes are tender. Season with pepper and stir in the mushrooms for the last 5 minutes of cooking. Sprinkle with the parsley and serve.

ONE SERVING	
CALORIES	250
TOTAL FAT	4g
SATURATED FAT	1g
CARBOHYDRATES	44g
ADDED SUGAR	0
FIBRE	5g
SODIUM	90mg

TIP
To peel the button onions, blanch them in a pan of boiling water for 3 minutes, then cool slightly. Gently remove the skins, leaving the root end intact so that the onions remain whole.

Whole button onions add a hint of sweetness to this warming winter stew, thickened and coloured by the lentils which absorb its hearty flavour as they swell.

Noodle and tofu stir-fry

SERVES 4
*PREPARATION TIME: 15 minutes, plus 20 minutes
to marinate*
COOKING TIME: 20 minutes

*1 tablespoon each soy sauce, dry sherry
and sesame oil*
8oz (225g) firm tofu, cut into cubes
4oz (115g) Chinese egg noodles
1 tablespoon olive oil
2 cloves garlic, peeled and chopped
1 level teaspoon peeled and grated root ginger
*8 medium spring onions, trimmed and cut
into short lengths*
2 carrots, peeled and thinly sliced
2 sticks celery, trimmed and thinly sliced
*8oz (225g) broccoli, trimmed and divided
into florets*
4oz (115g) mushrooms, wiped and sliced
8fl oz (225ml) vegetable stock
1 level tablespoon cornflour

ONE SERVING

CALORIES 280

TOTAL FAT 13g

SATURATED FAT 1g

CARBOHYDRATES 29g

ADDED SUGAR 0

FIBRE 4g

SODIUM 355mg

1 Mix the soy sauce, sherry and sesame oil
in a shallow dish. Put in the tofu and turn it
gently to coat the cubes, then cover and leave
to marinate for 20 minutes.

2 Cook the noodles in unsalted water
drain and set aside.

3 Heat the olive oil in a wok or a large,
heavy-based saucepan and stir-fry the garlic,
ginger, onions, carrots and celery in it over a
high heat for 2 minutes. Stir in the broccoli,
mushrooms and half the stock, then lower the
heat, cover and simmer for 3 minutes.

4 Drain the marinade off the tofu into a
small bowl and blend in the cornflour. Stir in
the remaining stock, pour onto the vegetables
and cook, stirring constantly, until thickened.

5 Mix in the noodles and tofu, cover and
simmer for 3-4 minutes, until heated through.

*Tofu, a mild, cheese-like curd made from soya beans,
soaks up the flavours of the Orient in this medley of
crisp vegetables, soft noodles and sharp sauce.*

Sunflower seeds give a crunchy topping to this moist and chewy roast of mixed nuts and vegetables, which is bound with eggs and easy to make.

Nut roast

ONE SERVING

CALORIES 270

TOTAL FAT 16g

SATURATED FAT 2g

CARBOHYDRATES 21g

ADDED SUGAR 0

FIBRE 4g

SODIUM 230mg

SERVES 4
PREPARATION TIME: 20 minutes
COOKING TIME: 1 hour 15 minutes
OVEN: Preheat to 180°C (350°F, gas mark 4)

2 medium onions, peeled and finely chopped
1 small green pepper, de-seeded and finely chopped
3 sticks celery, trimmed and finely chopped
1 carrot, peeled and grated
3oz (85g) unsalted mixed nuts (cashews, hazelnuts, peanuts, almonds), finely chopped
4oz (115g) wholemeal breadcrumbs
1 level teaspoon dried mixed herbs
Freshly ground black pepper
2 eggs, size 2, lightly beaten
1 tablespoon tomato purée
1 level tablespoon sunflower seeds

1 Mix the onions, green pepper, celery, carrot, nuts, breadcrumbs and mixed herbs in a bowl.

Season with black pepper, then work in the eggs and tomato purée to bind the mixture.

2 Spoon the mixture into a lightly oiled nonstick loaf tin about 8×4in (20×10cm) and press it down firmly with the back of the spoon. Sprinkle the sunflower seeds evenly over the mixture.

3 Cook the roast in the heated oven for about 1 hour 15 minutes, or until the top is crisp and a skewer inserted into the centre comes out clean. Ease the sides of the roast gently away from the tin with a round-ended knife. Turn the loaf out carefully onto a board, and then turn again onto a warmed serving plate with the sunflower seeds uppermost.

Vegetable paella with eggs

ONE SERVING

CALORIES 370

TOTAL FAT 11g

SATURATED FAT 2g

CARBOHYDRATES 57g

ADDED SUGAR 0

FIBRE 6g

SODIUM 120mg

Eggs replace the traditional seafood and chicken in this version of the Spanish paella. The result is a colourful dish built round the creamy-textured rice.

SERVES 4
PREPARATION TIME: 20 minutes
COOKING TIME: 35 minutes

1 tablespoon olive oil
1 medium onion, peeled and chopped
1 clove garlic, peeled and finely chopped
1 level teaspoon paprika
¼ level teaspoon cayenne pepper
1 small red pepper, de-seeded and cut into strips
1 medium yellow pepper, de-seeded and cut into strips
4 medium tomatoes, skinned and chopped
2 small potatoes, peeled and diced
2 medium carrots, peeled and cut into strips
7oz (200g) Valencia or long-grain rice
⅛ level teaspoon salt
1 pint (570ml) vegetable stock
2 medium courgettes, quartered and thickly sliced
8oz (225g) frozen peas

3 eggs, size 2, hard-boiled, shelled and quartered
1 level tablespoon chopped fresh parsley

1 Heat the oil in a large, heavy-based saucepan and gently fry the onion and garlic in it for 5 minutes. Add the paprika, cayenne, peppers and tomatoes, and cook for 2 minutes, stirring.

2 Mix in the potatoes, carrots, rice and salt, pour in the stock and bring to the boil. Cover and simmer for 15 minutes, until most of the liquid is absorbed.

3 Stir in the courgettes and peas, and simmer for a further 10 minutes, then turn out onto a heated serving dish. Arrange the eggs round the paella and sprinkle the parsley over the top.

Serve a mixed leafy salad to add crispness and fresh colour to the tender paella.

> **TIP**
> *Use Valencia rice, when you can get it, for the authentic texture of paella. The rice is short-grained and readily absorbs the cooking liquid to become plump and moist, but not sticky.*

Pancakes with Mexican stuffing

ONE SERVING

CALORIES 545

TOTAL FAT 15g

SATURATED FAT 5g

CARBOHYDRATES 75g

ADDED SUGAR 0

FIBRE 10g

SODIUM 320mg

SERVES 4
PREPARATION TIME: 1 hour 30 minutes
COOKING TIME: 30 minutes
OVEN: Preheat to 190°C (375°F, gas mark 5)

8oz (225g) plain flour
2 eggs, size 2, lightly beaten

¾ pint (425ml) skimmed milk
1 medium onion, peeled and finely chopped
1 clove garlic, peeled and crushed
1lb (450g) tomatoes, skinned and chopped
1 level teaspoon cumin seeds
2 teaspoons tomato purée
12oz (340g) cooked red kidney beans

4oz (115g) cooked black-eyed beans
4 teaspoons corn oil
Greaseproof paper squares for layering pancakes
4oz (115g) grated reduced-fat Cheddar cheese
Flat-leaf parsley sprigs to garnish

1 Sift the flour into a bowl, make a well in the centre and pour in the eggs. Whisk the eggs into the flour, adding milk little by little to form a thick, smooth batter. Stir in the rest of the milk, pour the batter into a large measuring jug, cover and leave to stand for 30 minutes.

2 Simmer the onion, garlic, tomatoes, cumin seeds and tomato purée in an uncovered saucepan for about 15 minutes, until the onion is tender and the mixture slightly thickened.

3 Mash all the beans roughly in a large bowl, then stir in the tomato mixture.

4 Heat ½ teaspoon of the oil over a moderate heat in a nonstick frying pan 8in (20cm) in diameter. Pour in an eighth of the batter and run it round the pan to coat the base. Cook for 2-3 minutes and when it is opaque on the surface and lightly browned underneath, flip it over with a fish slice. Cook the other side for 2 minutes until golden. Tip the pancake onto a lightly oiled plate, with the side cooked first underneath. Put a piece of greaseproof paper on top. Make 7 more pancakes in the same way.

5 Spoon a share of the filling onto the top pancake in the pile, roll it up and put it seam down in a greased shallow ovenproof dish. Fill the other pancakes and put them in the dish.

6 Sprinkle the Cheddar over the pancakes. Cover the dish and cook in the heated oven for 10 minutes, then uncover and cook for another 20 minutes, until browned on top.

Serve the pancakes garnished with parsley sprigs and accompanied by a light, leafy salad. You can make the pancakes a day in advance and instead of filling them, wait until they are cold, wrap them in a polythene bag and store them in the refrigerator.

A tomato and bean filling, well flavoured with garlic, onion and cumin seeds, gives these cheese-topped pancakes their spicy Mexican character.

Pancakes oriental style

SERVES 4
PREPARATION TIME: 1 hour
COOKING TIME: 1 hour 5 minutes

ONE SERVING	
CALORIES 485	
TOTAL FAT 21g	
SATURATED FAT 3g	
CARBOHYDRATES 58g	
ADDED SUGAR 0	
FIBRE 3g	
SODIUM 385mg	

TIP
To make a spring onion curl, trim off the base and all but 2in (50mm) of the green leaves. Make several cuts down the leaves and just into the white part. Put into ice-cold water, refrigerate for 30 minutes and the leaves will curl back.

2 level tablespoons chopped fresh coriander leaves
8oz (225g) plain flour
1 egg, size 2, beaten
1 pint (570ml) skimmed milk
1 tablespoon soy sauce
1 teaspoon sesame oil
1 level tablespoon peeled and grated root ginger
1 clove garlic, peeled and crushed
8oz (225g) firm tofu, cut into small cubes
½ oz (15g) dried shiitake mushrooms
2 tablespoons corn oil
Greaseproof paper squares for layering pancakes
1 red pepper, de-seeded and finely diced
4 spring onions, trimmed and finely sliced
2oz (60g) sugar snap peas or mangetout, trimmed and halved
1oz (30g) blanched almonds, cut into thin slivers
1 large spring onion, trimmed, quartered lengthways and separated into strands
Spring onion curls to garnish

1 Put the coriander and flour into a large bowl, make a well in the centre and pour the egg into it. Whisk vigorously, adding milk a little at a time to form a thick, smooth batter. Stir in the rest of the milk, pour the batter into a large measuring jug, cover and leave to stand for 30 minutes.

2 Meanwhile, mix the soy sauce, sesame oil, ginger and garlic in a shallow dish. Put the tofu in the dish, spoon the mixture over the cubes to coat them, then cover and leave to marinate for 1 hour.

3 Rinse the mushrooms well, put them in a bowl and pour on ¼ pint (150ml) of water, just off the boil. Leave to stand for 30 minutes.

4 Heat a scant ½ teaspoon of the corn oil over a moderate heat in a nonstick frying pan 8in (20cm) in diameter. Pour in a twelfth of the batter, tilting the pan until the base is coated with a very thin layer. Cook for 2-3 minutes, or until the pancake is opaque on the surface and lightly browned underneath. Flip it over with a fish slice and cook the other side for 1-2 minutes until lightly browned. Tip the pancake out of the pan onto an oiled plate, with the side that was cooked first underneath. Put a piece of greaseproof paper on top. Make 11 more pancakes in the same way.

5 Drain the mushrooms and chop them finely. Drain the tofu, reserving the marinade. Heat the remaining drops of corn oil in a wok or large frying pan. Stir-fry the red pepper, sliced spring onions and mushrooms in it over a high heat for 2 minutes. Stir in the peas and almonds and cook for 2 minutes. Reduce the heat, spoon in the tofu carefully and heat through gently for 2-3 minutes. Pour in the reserved marinade and bring to the boil.

6 Spoon equal amounts of the filling onto each pancake. Carefully bring the edges together above the filling to form a small 'purse' and tie with a strand of spring onion.

7 Put the pancakes onto two lightly greased plates, cover with upturned heatproof dishes and steam over pans of simmering water for 5 minutes, to heat through. If you have a bamboo or tiered steamer, line it with nonstick baking paper and heat the pancakes in it.

Lift the pancakes carefully onto heated plates and garnish with spring onion curls. Serve with a salad of bean sprouts and lamb's lettuce, and side dishes of spring onion slivers. It is often more convenient to make the pancakes a day in advance. Stack with greaseproof paper between them, and instead of filling them, wait until they are cold, put them in a polythene bag and store in the refrigerator.

Pancake purses are plump with an assortment of crisp, colourful stir-fried vegetables and tofu flavoured with soy sauce, sesame oil and ginger. The purses, speckled with aromatic coriander, are steamed at the end of cooking, keeping them moist and the fillings warm and tender.

Peppers with bean and mushroom filling

SERVES 4
PREPARATION TIME: 55 minutes
COOKING TIME: 25 minutes
OVEN: Preheat to 190°C (375°F, gas mark 5)

ONE SERVING	
CALORIES 345	
TOTAL FAT 16g	
SATURATED FAT 3g	
CARBOHYDRATES 41g	
ADDED SUGAR 0	
FIBRE 8g	
SODIUM 125mg	

TIP
When fresh broad beans are reaching the end of their season, their grey-green skin may be tough and slightly bitter. Pull the skin off the beans so that it does not spoil the filling.

2 medium onions, peeled and finely chopped
1 pint (570ml) vegetable stock
4oz (115g) mushrooms, wiped and chopped
1 clove garlic, peeled and finely chopped
4oz (115g) brown rice
1lb (450g) tomatoes, skinned and chopped
2 level tablespoons chopped fresh parsley
1 tablespoon olive oil
1 level teaspoon each ground cumin
and ground coriander
1 red pepper, de-seeded and cut into strips
4 green peppers, each about 7oz (200g),
halved lengthways and de-seeded
2oz (60g) shelled and chopped walnuts
2oz (60g) shelled fresh broad beans or frozen
broad beans
Freshly ground black pepper
2oz (60g) grated mature Cheddar cheese

1 Put half the onion into a saucepan with 2 tablespoons of the stock, the mushrooms and garlic, and cook for 3-4 minutes over a moderate heat, stirring occasionally. Pour in the rice and cook for 2-3 minutes.

2 Stir about one-third of the tomatoes, all the parsley and ¾ pint (425ml) of the stock into the pan. Bring to the boil, cover and simmer for about 30 minutes, until the rice is tender and the liquid has been absorbed.

3 Meanwhile, heat the oil in a frying pan and fry the remaining onion in it for about 5 minutes, until golden. Sprinkle in the cumin and coriander, and cook for 1 minute.

4 Stir the remaining tomatoes and stock and the red pepper into the frying pan. Bring to the boil, then simmer for about 15 minutes, until the liquid is reduced and the mixture slightly thickened. Pass the mixture through a food mill or sieve, or cool it slightly and blend in a food processor to make a smooth sauce.

Broad beans, chewy brown rice and walnuts are moistened by mushrooms and packed into sweet peppers, which are served in a spiced tomato sauce.

5 Blanch the green pepper halves in boiling water for 4 minutes and drain. Arrange the peppers, cut side up, in a single layer in a baking dish.

6 Stir the walnuts and beans into the rice mixture, season it with pepper and pack it into the peppers. Cover and cook in the heated oven for about 15 minutes, then uncover, sprinkle with the Cheddar and cook for 10 minutes more, until the peppers are tender but not collapsing, and the cheese has melted.

7 Reheat the sauce and pour it round the peppers before taking them to the table.

Tofu and vegetable stir-fry with rice

ONE SERVING

CALORIES 455

TOTAL FAT 17g

SATURATED FAT 1g

CARBOHYDRATES 61g

ADDED SUGAR 0

FIBRE 3g

SODIUM 315mg

SERVES 4
PREPARATION TIME: 15 minutes, plus 1 hour
to marinate
COOKING TIME: 20 minutes

1 level tablespoon peeled and grated root ginger
2½ tablespoons sesame oil
2 cloves garlic, peeled and crushed
1 tablespoon soy sauce

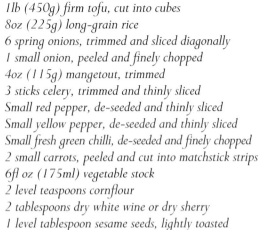

1lb (450g) firm tofu, cut into cubes
8oz (225g) long-grain rice
6 spring onions, trimmed and sliced diagonally
1 small onion, peeled and finely chopped
4oz (115g) mangetout, trimmed
3 sticks celery, trimmed and thinly sliced
Small red pepper, de-seeded and thinly sliced
Small yellow pepper, de-seeded and thinly sliced
Small fresh green chilli, de-seeded and finely chopped
2 small carrots, peeled and cut into matchstick strips
6fl oz (175ml) vegetable stock
2 level teaspoons cornflour
2 tablespoons dry white wine or dry sherry
1 level tablespoon sesame seeds, lightly toasted

1 Mix half the ginger, 1 tablespoon of the oil,
half the garlic and the soy sauce in a shallow
dish. Put in the tofu and turn gently to coat the
cubes. Cover and put in the refrigerator to
marinate for 1 hour. Fifteen minutes before the
hour is up, start cooking the rice.

2 While the rice is cooking, heat 1 tablespoon
of the remaining oil in a wok or large frying
pan. Stir-fry the spring onions and the rest of
the ginger and garlic in it over a high heat for
30 seconds, then mix in the chopped onion,
mangetout, celery, peppers and chilli, and
stir-fry for 2-3 minutes.

3 Stir in the carrots and half the stock, then
add the tofu and its marinade. Lower the heat,
cover and simmer for 3-4 minutes, until the
vegetables are just cooked but firm.

4 Meanwhile, blend the cornflour with the
remaining sesame oil and mix with the wine or
sherry and the rest of the stock. Pour into the
wok or pan and stir carefully over a moderate
heat for 2-3 minutes, until the sauce thickens.
Take care not to break up the tofu.

5 Pile the rice onto a heated serving dish,
spoon the tofu and vegetable mixture on top
and sprinkle with the sesame seeds.

Serve a salad of lamb's lettuce and watercress to
provide a sharp contrast to the stir-fry.

*Mild tofu readily soaks up the strong flavours of a
ginger, sesame oil and soy sauce marinade, making it
a welcome addition to this vegetable stir-fry.*

Two-layer tortilla

SERVES 4
PREPARATION TIME: 20 minutes
COOKING TIME: 10 minutes
OVEN: Preheat to 120°C (250°F, gas mark ½)

ONE SERVING

CALORIES 425

TOTAL FAT 22g

SATURATED FAT 4g

CARBOHYDRATES 20g

ADDED SUGAR 0

FIBRE 4g

SODIUM 300mg

1 tablespoon olive oil
1 medium onion, peeled and chopped
¾ pint (425ml) tomato sauce
6 eggs, size 2
4oz (115g) frozen leaf spinach, thawed
12oz (340g) potatoes, boiled but firm, diced
Freshly ground black pepper
1 level tablespoon chopped fresh parsley

1 Heat the oil in a frying pan and gently cook the onion in it for 10 minutes, until softened. Put the tomato sauce to simmer in a small pan.

2 Break 3 eggs into each of two bowls and beat lightly. Mix the spinach into one bowl and the potato into the other. Mix half the onion into each bowl and season with pepper.

3 Heat the grill to high. Heat a nonstick omelette pan 8in (20cm) in diameter. Pour in the spinach mixture and spread it evenly in the pan. Cook gently for about 4 minutes, until the mixture comes away easily from the sides. Put under the grill for 1-2 minutes to set the top. Slide from the pan onto a warm serving plate and spoon on half the tomato sauce. Cover and put in the heated oven.

4 Cook the potato mixture in the same way. Slide it on top of the spinach tortilla, and spoon the remaining tomato sauce on top. Sprinkle with the parsley.

Serve the tortilla with sprigs of parsley to garnish, if you like, and with plenty of bread.

TIP
If you have no grill to cook the top of each tortilla, put a large plate over the pan and turn pan and plate over together so that the tortilla is on the plate. Carefully slide it back into the pan to cook the other side.

The name 'tortilla' shows that Spain is the source of this layered omelette. You can vary the vegetable additions, but potato is one of the best as it makes the dish more filling.

Spinach ring with white-bean sauce

SERVES 4
PREPARATION TIME: 20 minutes
COOKING TIME: 45 minutes
OVEN: Preheat to 180°C (350°F, gas mark 4)

1lb (450g) fresh spinach, trimmed, washed and shredded
½ oz (15g) polyunsaturated margarine
2 level tablespoons plain flour
¼ pint (150ml) skimmed milk
1oz (30g) grated Parmesan cheese
1 egg, separated, plus 1 egg white, size 2
11oz (300g) cooked butter beans, or haricot or lima beans
2 tablespoons olive oil
2 level tablespoons low-fat natural yoghurt
1 tablespoon lemon juice
⅛ level teaspoon salt
⅛ level teaspoon cayenne pepper
¼ pint (150ml) vegetable stock
Watercress to garnish

ONE SERVING	
CALORIES	440
TOTAL FAT	17g
SATURATED FAT	4g
CARBOHYDRATES	47g
ADDED SUGAR	0
FIBRE	16g
SODIUM	612mg

1 Put the spinach in a large saucepan without any water, cover and cook it for 2 minutes over a moderate heat in the juice that runs from it. Take off the lid and continue cooking, stirring often, for about 4 minutes, until the spinach is just tender. Drain off any remaining juice.

2 Melt the butter in a medium saucepan over a low heat, stir in the flour and gradually mix in the milk. Bring to the boil, stirring, then simmer for 2 minutes until the sauce thickens. Remove the pan from the heat and stir in the Parmesan, the egg yolk and the spinach.

3 Grease a 1 pint (570ml) ring mould and toss a little flour round in it to coat it; shake out the excess. Whisk the egg whites until they will hold soft peaks and use a metal spoon to fold them gently into the spinach mixture. Pour into the mould and spread evenly. Cook in the heated oven for about 40 minutes, until the spinach ring is well risen and feels firm when pressed lightly with a fingertip.

4 Meanwhile, blend the beans, oil, yoghurt, lemon juice, salt, cayenne pepper and vegetable stock in a food processor until smooth. Pour into a saucepan.

5 When the spinach ring is ready, take it out of the oven and let it cool in the tin for 5 minutes. Meanwhile, stir the bean sauce over a moderate heat until hot, but do not let it boil. Pour the sauce into a heated serving jug.

6 Run a knife round the inner and outer rim of the spinach ring and turn it out onto a warmed serving plate. Garnish it with the watercress and serve at once, handing round the sauce separately.

The dish is a substantial one, but you may like some wholemeal or herb-flavoured rolls and a tomato salad with it.

A creamy sauce combined with dark green spinach creates this attractive ring. Egg whites fluff it into a light and airy partner for a rich white-bean purée.

This highly spiced dish, reminiscent of traditional North African dishes, is served on a fluffy bed of couscous, granules made from wheat.

Spiced vegetable stew with couscous

ONE SERVING	
CALORIES	360
TOTAL FAT	7g
SATURATED FAT	1g
CARBOHYDRATES	62g
ADDED SUGAR	0
FIBRE	7g
SODIUM	160mg

SERVES 4
PREPARATION TIME: 15 minutes
COOKING TIME: 25 minutes

1 small cauliflower, trimmed and divided into florets
1 tablespoon olive oil
1 medium onion, peeled and chopped
3 cloves garlic, peeled and crushed
1 level teaspoon each turmeric, ground ginger, paprika
½ level teaspoon chilli powder
1¾ lb (800g) tinned chopped tomatoes
1 red pepper, de-seeded and thickly sliced
1 carrot, peeled and thinly sliced
2oz (60g) stoned prunes, halved
¼ pint (150ml) vegetable stock
1 cinnamon stick
6oz (175g) runner beans, strings removed, sliced
8oz (225g) cooked chickpeas
8oz (225g) couscous
16fl oz (485ml) boiling water
⅛ level teaspoon salt
Freshly ground black pepper

1 Blanch the cauliflower in boiling unsalted water for 2 minutes, drain and set aside.

2 Heat the oil in a large, heavy-based frying pan and cook the onion and garlic in it over a moderate heat for 5 minutes, until the onion colours. Add the turmeric, ginger, paprika and chilli powder, and fry for 30 seconds more.

3 Stir in the tomatoes, red pepper, carrot, prunes and stock, and put in the cinnamon stick. Cover and cook for 15 minutes. Mix in the cauliflower, beans and chickpeas, and cook for a further 5 minutes.

4 Meanwhile, put the couscous into a bowl with the boiling water. Stir, cover the bowl and leave to stand for about 15 minutes, or until the water has been absorbed. Season the couscous with the salt and black pepper and fluff it up with a fork.

5 Pile the couscous onto a warmed serving dish. Remove the cinnamon stick from the stew and spoon the stew over the couscous.

You can garnish the stew with mint sprigs or pale celery leaves, and serve warm rolls with it.

Pizza with three-pepper topping

SERVES 4
PREPARATION TIME: 30 minutes,
plus 45 minutes to rise
COOKING TIME: 25 minutes
OVEN: Preheat to 220°C (425°F, gas mark 7)

ONE SERVING

CALORIES 440

TOTAL FAT 20g

SATURATED FAT 5g

CARBOHYDRATES 51g

ADDED SUGAR 0

FIBRE 6g

SODIUM 375mg

¼ pint (150ml) lukewarm water
½ level teaspoon caster sugar
1 level teaspoon dried yeast
4oz (115g) plain flour
4oz (115g) wholemeal flour
3½ tablespoons olive oil
3 small peppers, green, red and yellow,
de-seeded and sliced into rings
1 medium onion, peeled and chopped
14oz (400g) tinned tomatoes, drained
and chopped
2 cloves garlic, peeled and crushed
2 level teaspoons dried oregano
1 level tablespoon chopped fresh basil
Freshly ground black pepper
4oz (115g) mozzarella or low-fat
Cheddar cheese, grated
8 black olives, stoned and quartered
Fresh basil leaves to garnish

1 Pour the water into a small bowl, stir in the sugar until dissolved, then whisk in the yeast. Cover and leave to stand in a warm place for 10 minutes, until frothy.

2 Mix the plain and wholemeal flour in a bowl, make a well in the centre and pour in 2 tablespoons of the oil and all the yeast liquid. Mix to form a dough, then knead on a floured surface for about 5 minutes, until even-textured, springy and no longer sticky. Put the dough in a clean bowl, cover and set in a warm place – for example, in an airing cupboard or near a hot radiator. Leave to rise for 45 minutes, or until the dough has doubled in size.

3 Meanwhile, heat 1 tablespoon of the remaining oil in a frying pan and cook the peppers in it for 5 minutes over a moderate heat, until they start to soften. Spoon out the peppers and set them aside.

4 Stir the onion, tomatoes, garlic, oregano and basil into the pan and season with black pepper. Bring to the boil, reduce the heat and simmer for 10 minutes, stirring frequently, until the sauce has thickened slightly. Remove from the heat and leave to cool.

5 Knead the risen dough for 2-3 minutes, then roll it into a circle 10in (25cm) in diameter and lay it in a pizza tin or on a baking sheet greased with a little of the remaining oil. Brush the rest of the oil over the dough.

6 Spread the tomato sauce over the dough, leaving ½ in (13mm) clear round the rim. Spoon the green, red and yellow peppers over the sauce, then sprinkle with the mozzarella or Cheddar. Arrange the olives on top and cook the pizza in the heated oven for 20-25 minutes, until the base is crisp and the cheese melted and beginning to brown. Scatter on the garnish of basil leaves.

Serve a crisp, leafy salad with the pizza to make a sharp contrast with the colour and texture of the soft, sweet-pepper topping.

TIP
You can save time by using quick-acting yeast to make the pizza base. Or you can plan ahead and prepare a larger batch of dough, making enough for three pizza bases and freezing two after they are rolled out.

A combination of brown and white flours produces a plump, puffy pizza base with a nutty, wholesome flavour. Red, yellow and green pepper rings make a colourful and intricate topping to stud with savoury pieces of olive. A thick, spicy tomato sauce and melted strands of cheese complete the Italian mood.

Asparagus baked in white wine

SERVES 4
PREPARATION TIME: 5 minutes
COOKING TIME: 20 minutes
OVEN: Preheat to 180°C (350°F, gas mark 4)

ONE SERVING
CALORIES 70
TOTAL FAT 5g
  SATURATED FAT 3g
CARBOHYDRATES 2g
  ADDED SUGAR 0
FIBRE 2g
SODIUM 6mg

1lb (450g) fresh asparagus, trimmed and
stalks peeled
5fl oz (150ml) dry white wine
3 tablespoons double cream
1/8 level teaspoon paprika

1 Put the asparagus in a shallow casserole dish
with all the tips pointing the same way.

2 Pour in the wine, cover with a tightly
fitting lid or foil, and bake in the heated oven
for 15 minutes. Carefully turn the asparagus
once during cooking.

3 When the asparagus is just tender, stir in
the cream until well blended, taking care not to
damage the delicate tips. Return to the oven
and bake for 5 minutes.

4 Stir the sauce again just before serving and
sprinkle the stalk ends of the asparagus with a
dusting of paprika.

TIP
*Use a potato peeler
to pare off the
outermost skin of
the bottom half of
the asparagus
stalks. This ensures
that the stalks cook
as fast as the tips.*

*Bathed in a creamy
wine sauce, delicate
young asparagus makes
a simple, delicious treat
for family or guests.*

Aubergine and pumpkin gratin

ONE SERVING
CALORIES 75
TOTAL FAT 4g
  SATURATED FAT 1g
CARBOHYDRATES 6g
  ADDED SUGAR 0
FIBRE 4g
SODIUM 8mg

SERVES 4
PREPARATION TIME: 15 minutes
COOKING TIME: 25 minutes

1 tablespoon olive oil
1 clove garlic, peeled and crushed
1 small onion, peeled and finely chopped
2 tablespoons water
1 bay leaf
2 level teaspoons chopped fresh rosemary, or 1 level
teaspoon dried rosemary
4 chopped fresh sage leaves

1lb (450g) pumpkin, peeled, de-seeded and cubed
1lb (450g) aubergine, cut into cubes
2 level tablespoons Greek yoghurt
2 teaspoons lemon juice
1 level tablespoon chopped fresh parsley
Freshly ground black pepper
Sage sprig to garnish

1 Heat the oil in a large, nonstick frying pan
and put in the garlic, onion and water. Cook
over a moderate heat for 2 minutes, or until the
water has evaporated.

2 Add the bay leaf, rosemary and sage, and cook for 1 minute, then stir in the pumpkin and aubergine. Cover and cook over a low heat, stirring occasionally, for about 15 minutes, or until the vegetables are tender.

3 Take the pan off the heat, discard the bay leaf, stir in the yoghurt, lemon juice and parsley, and season with pepper. Turn into a heatproof dish and brown under a hot grill for 5 minutes. Garnish with the sage sprig.

Aubergine and tomato slices

SERVES 4
PREPARATION TIME: 10 minutes
COOKING TIME: 20 minutes
OVEN: Preheat to 190°C (375°F, gas mark 5)

ONE SERVING

CALORIES 60

TOTAL FAT 5g

SATURATED FAT 1g

CARBOHYDRATES 3g

ADDED SUGAR 0

FIBRE 2g

SODIUM 5mg

1 medium aubergine, trimmed and cut into 8 thick slices
1½ tablespoons olive oil
2 small ripe tomatoes, each cut into 4 slices
2 level tablespoons chopped fresh basil, or 1 level teaspoon dried basil
Freshly ground black pepper
8 fresh basil leaves to garnish

1 Arrange the aubergine slices in a single layer on a nonstick baking sheet and bake in the heated oven for 15 minutes, or until tender.

2 Brush the aubergine slices with half the oil and lay a slice of tomato on top of each one. Trickle on the remaining oil, sprinkle the chopped basil on top and season with pepper.

3 Put the baking sheet under the grill, and cook under a medium heat for 6 minutes, or until the tomatoes are soft. Garnish each aubergine slice with a basil leaf for serving.

Colourful, adaptable aubergines can be gently softened with golden pumpkin cubes and flavoured with herbs before being browned under the grill. They are equally good when sliced and baked in olive oil before being topped with tomato rounds and spicy basil.

Two-potato cake

ONE SERVING

CALORIES 195

TOTAL FAT 6g

SATURATED FAT 1g

CARBOHYDRATES 34g

ADDED SUGAR 0

FIBRE 3g

SODIUM 155mg

SERVES 4
PREPARATION TIME: 15 minutes
COOKING TIME: 30 minutes

8fl oz (225ml) dry cider
⅛ level teaspoon salt
⅛ level teaspoon ground cloves
Freshly ground black pepper

1oz (30g) polyunsaturated margarine, melted
1lb (450g) baking potatoes, peeled and thinly sliced
12oz (340g) sweet potatoes, peeled and
thinly sliced
2 level tablespoons snipped fresh chives

1 Pour the cider into a saucepan, sprinkle in
the salt and cloves, and season with pepper.
Boil gently for about 5 minutes, until the cider
is reduced by half, then set aside.

2 Brush a deep nonstick frying pan about
8in (20cm) in diameter with melted margarine.
Cover the bottom of the pan with a third of the
potatoes, then trickle over them 1 teaspoon of
the margarine and 1½ tablespoons of the cider.
Cover the potatoes with half the sweet potatoes
and trickle on 1 teaspoon of the margarine and
1½ tablespoons of the cider. Repeat the layers,
then finish with the remaining potatoes and
trickle on the rest of the margarine and cider.

3 Cook the potato cake for about 5 minutes
over a moderate heat, until it starts to sizzle,
then turn down the heat, cover and simmer for
a further 20 minutes.

4 Take the lid off the pan, increase the heat
and cook for about 5 minutes, until the
potatoes are tender and all the liquid has been
absorbed. Shake the pan frequently to prevent
the potatoes from sticking.

5 Cover the pan with a large, warmed
heatproof plate. Protecting your hands with
oven gloves, turn pan and plate over together to
turn out the cake. If one or two potato slices
stick to the pan, lift them out carefully and put
them in place on the cake. Put the cake under a
hot grill to give it a crisp finish. Sprinkle on the
chives just before serving.

*Layers of sweet potato add a musky scent and
contrasting texture to this potato cake. A basting of
cider flavoured with cloves, melds the layers and
brings out the subtle fruity flavour.*

Grated lemon rind gives these spinach balls a delicate citrus flavour, while basil-flavoured tomato sauce completes an attractive side dish.

Spinach balls in tomato sauce

ONE SERVING

CALORIES 205

TOTAL FAT 9g

SATURATED FAT 2g

CARBOHYDRATES 17g

ADDED SUGAR 0

FIBRE 7g

SODIUM 450mg

TIP
To cool the spinach quickly, spread it in a shallow heatproof dish and stand it in a baking tin of cold water. Change the water after 2 minutes.

SERVES 4
PREPARATION TIME: 20 minutes, plus 20 minutes to cool and refrigerate
COOKING TIME: 30 minutes
OVEN: Preheat to 180°C (350°F, gas mark 4)

1½ tablespoons olive oil
2 medium onions, peeled and finely chopped
2lb (900g) fresh spinach, trimmed, washed and chopped, or 1lb (450g) frozen spinach, thawed
4 cloves garlic, peeled and crushed
2oz (60g) wholemeal breadcrumbs
Finely grated rind of 1 lemon
½ oz (15g) grated Parmesan cheese
1 egg, size 2, beaten
Freshly ground black pepper
14oz (400g) tinned tomatoes, rubbed through a sieve
2 level tablespoons chopped fresh basil

1 Heat 1 tablespoon of the oil in a wide saucepan and cook half the onion in it over a moderate heat for 5 minutes. Add the spinach and half the garlic, and cook for 2-3 minutes,

covered. Uncover, raise the heat and stir for 2 minutes, or until the liquid has evaporated.

2 Cool for 5 minutes, then mix in the breadcrumbs, lemon rind, Parmesan and egg. Season with pepper and divide into 16 portions. Shape into balls and put in an oiled ovenproof dish. Cover and refrigerate for 15 minutes.

3 Meanwhile, heat the remaining oil in a medium saucepan and cook the rest of the onion in it over a moderate heat for 5 minutes. Stir in the remaining garlic, the tomatoes and half the basil. Season with pepper, cover and simmer for 30 minutes, stirring occasionally.

4 Cook the spinach balls, covered, in the heated oven for 30 minutes. Pour the tomato sauce over them and sprinkle with the remaining basil before serving.

Sharp lemon juice and savoury garlic are suitably robust partners for the assertive flavour of spinach, and the combination makes a lively side dish for a light summer meal.

TIP
Blanching the spinach rids it of excess bitterness and helps it to keep its rich green colour during cooking.

Sautéed spinach with lemon and garlic

SERVES 4
PREPARATION TIME: 20 minutes
COOKING TIME: 10 minutes

1½ lb (680g) fresh spinach, trimmed and washed
1½ teaspoons olive oil
1 medium onion, peeled and finely chopped
1 large clove garlic, thinly sliced lengthways
Freshly ground mixed peppercorns
2 teaspoons lemon juice

1 Blanch the spinach in a pan of boiling unsalted water for 1 minute, then rinse with cold water and drain, pressing with a wooden spoon to remove as much liquid as possible.

2 Heat the oil in a nonstick saucepan and cook the onion and garlic in it, uncovered, over a moderate heat for about 5 minutes. Add the spinach, cover and cook for about 4 minutes, stirring frequently.

3 Season the spinach with pepper and the lemon juice, and toss well. Turn it into a warm dish and serve at once.

For a richer dish, you can leave out the lemon juice, season the spinach with freshly grated nutmeg and stir in 2 level tablespoons of Greek yoghurt just before serving. This goes particularly well with steamed or grilled fish.

ONE SERVING	
CALORIES	60
TOTAL FAT	3g
SATURATED FAT	0
CARBOHYDRATES	5g
ADDED SUGAR	0
FIBRE	4g
SODIUM	205mg